THIS JOURNAL
BELONGS TO:
I'm stuck!

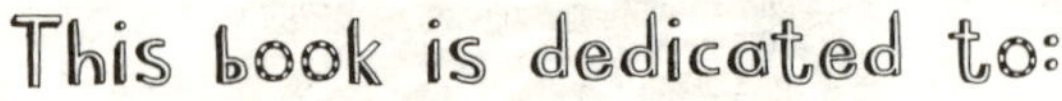

This book is dedicated to:

Toby and his mum, Zoe ♡

Isaac and his Aunty Wendy ♡

Zoë and her Aunty Lauren ♡

Hope you enjoy making this book your own!

♡

A very special THANK YOU to the wonderful Sheila Vaughan. Much love from me, Liz xx

Thank you to Team Scholastic, Lyn and Jason too ♡

SCHOLASTIC

Published in the UK by Scholastic, 2024
1 London Bridge, London, SE1 9BG
Scholastic Ireland, 89E Lagan Road, Dublin Industrial Estate,
Glasnevin, Dublin, D11 HP5F



ISBN 978-93-5954-419-9

A CIP catalogue record for this book is available from the British Library.



www.scholastic.co.uk

This reprint edition : August 2025

Printed by Acme Print o Pac Pvt Ltd Noida-201301

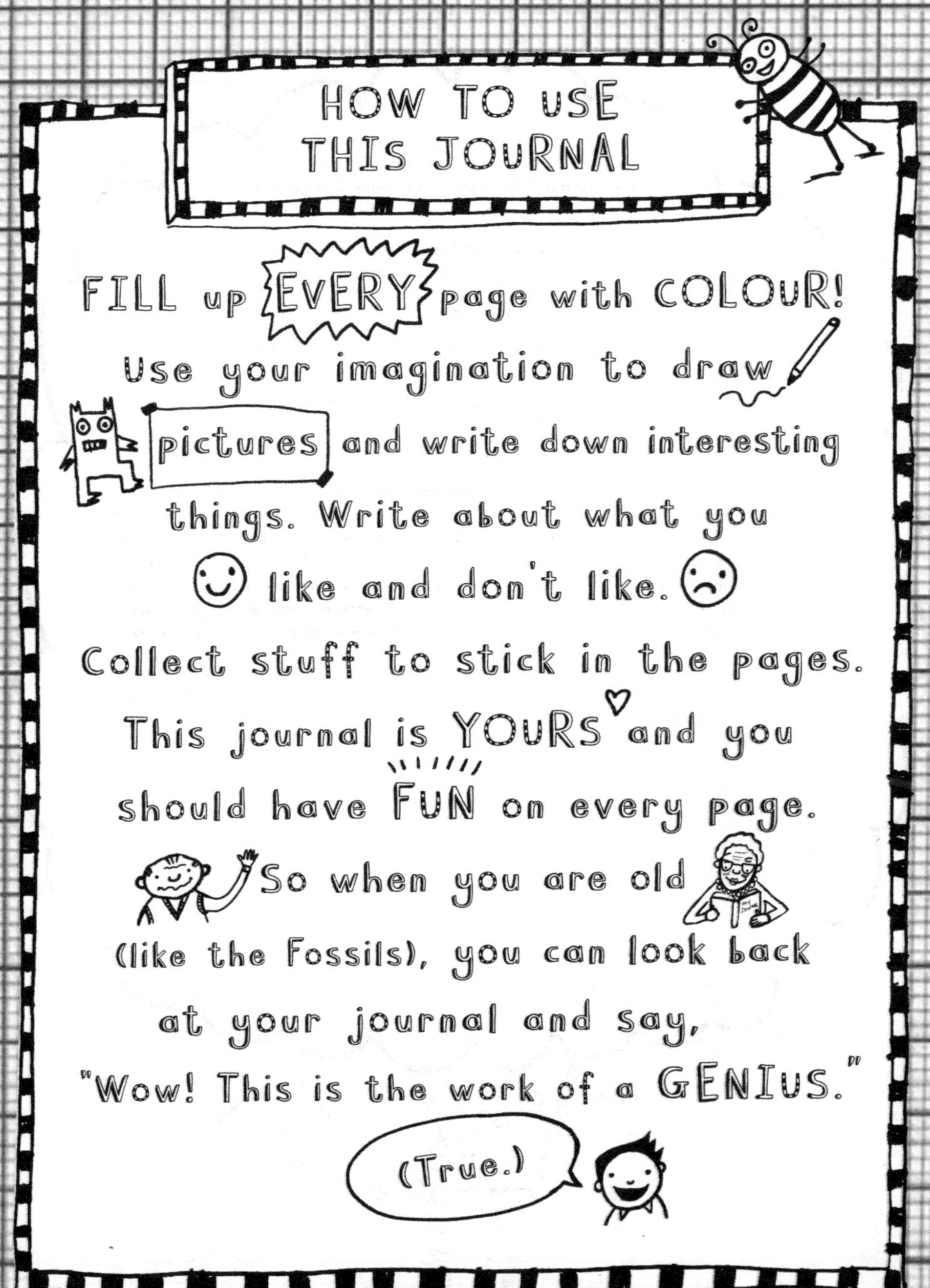
HOW TO USE THIS JOURNAL
FILL up EVERY page with COLOUR!
Use your imagination to draw pictures and write down interesting things. Write about what you like and don't like.
Collect stuff to stick in the pages.
This journal is YOURS and you should have FUN on every page.
So when you are old (like the Fossils), you can look back at your journal and say,
"Wow! This is the work of a GENIUS."
(True.)

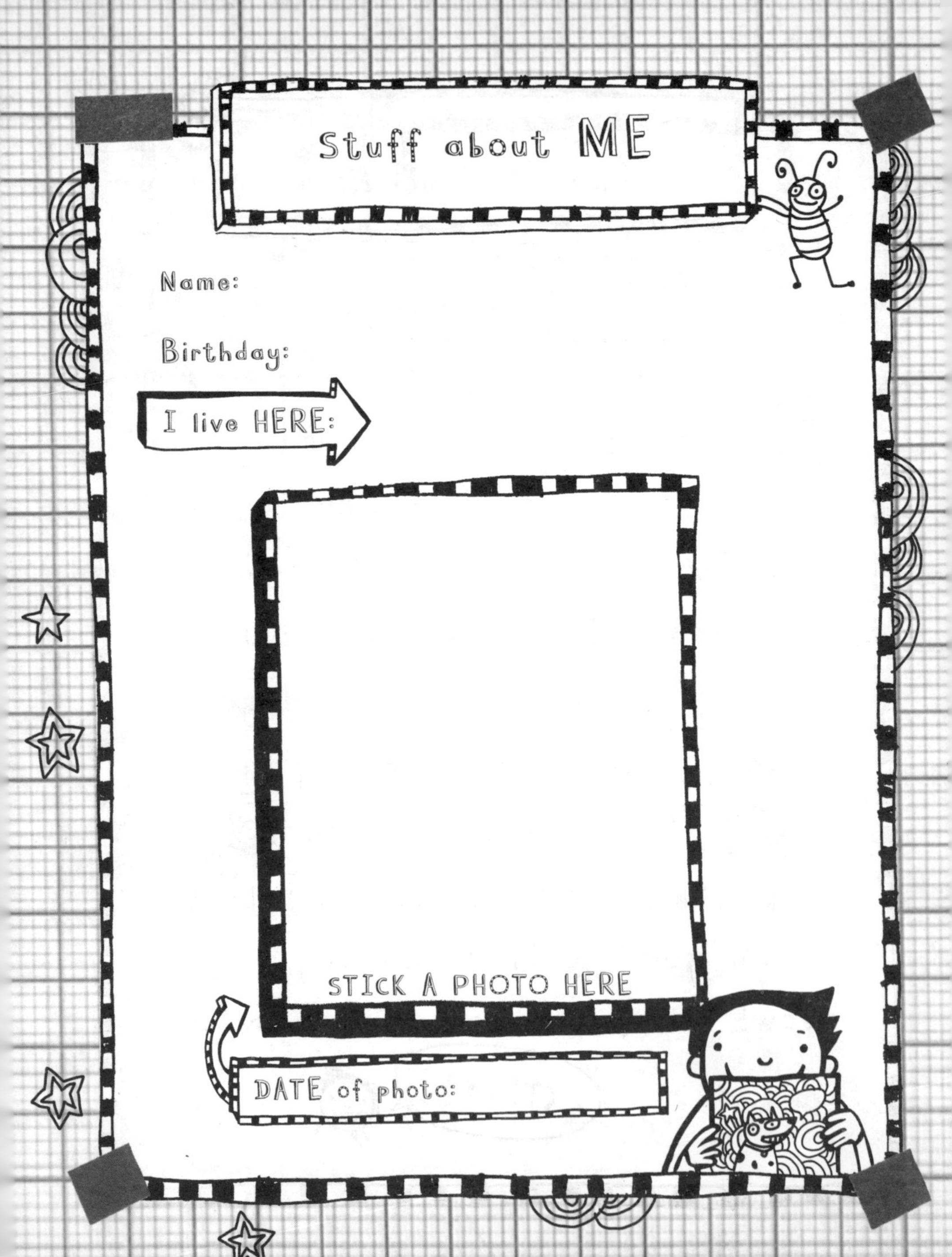
Stuff about ME
Name:
Birthday:
I live HERE:
STICK A PHOTO HERE
DATE of photo:

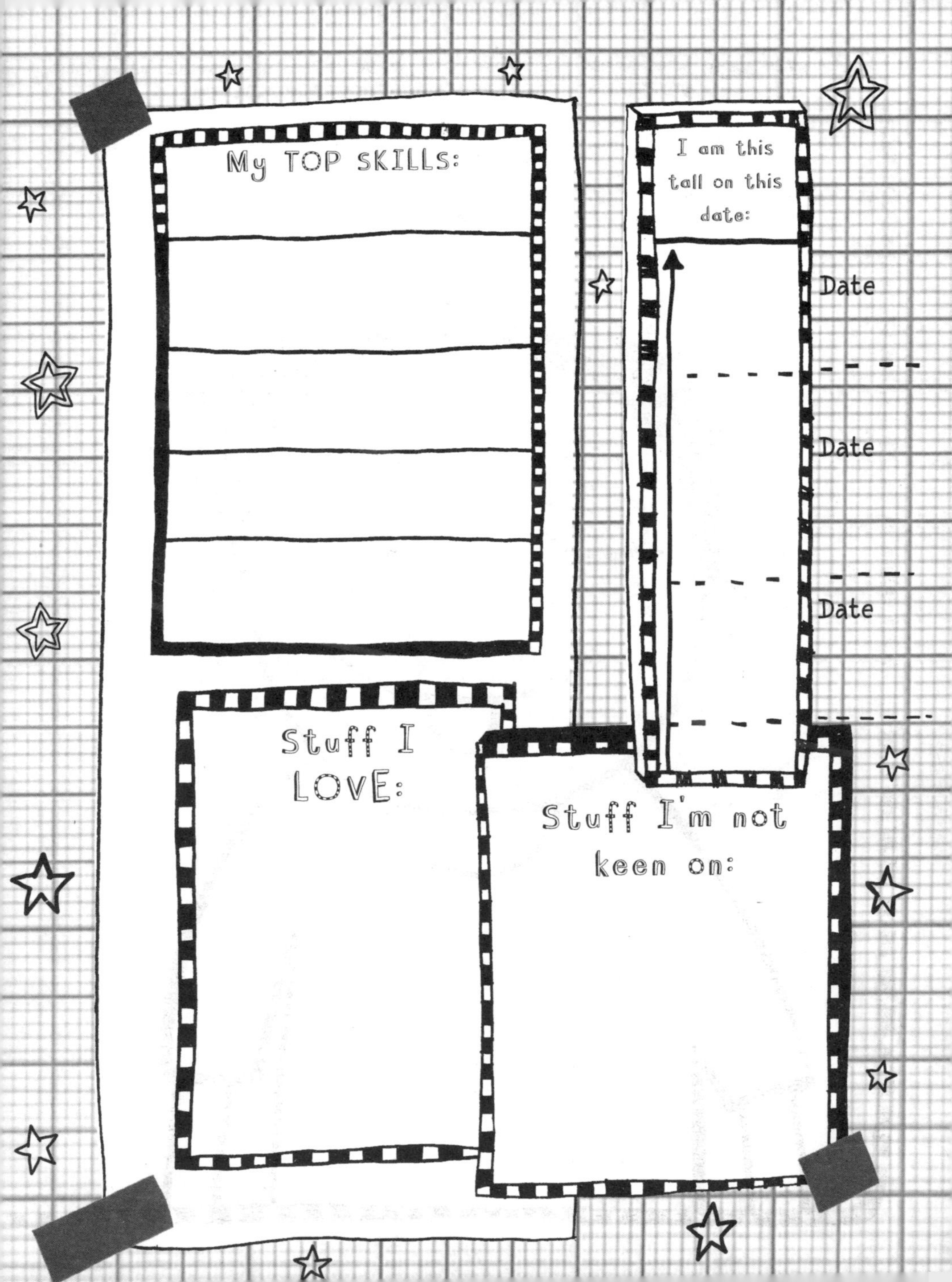
My TOP SKILLS:
I am this tall on this date:
Date
Date
Date
Stuff I LOVE:
Stuff I'm not keen on:

Draw a SILLY self-portrait

TOM

Write your name and DRAW lovely lines all round it.

TOM'S
TOP
5
JOKES
What's brown and sticky?
A stick.
Why was the maths book sad?
It had too many problems.
MATHS
4+12+8=?
Knock, knock! Who's there?
A little old lady.
Yodelee!
A little old lady who?
Nice yodelling.
What do you call a fish without an eye?
A FSH.
What did Caretaker Stan say when he jumped out of the stockroom?
"SUPPLIES!"

MY
TOP
5
JOKES

Free

STYLE

Stick your snack wrappers HERE!
FRUIT CHEW

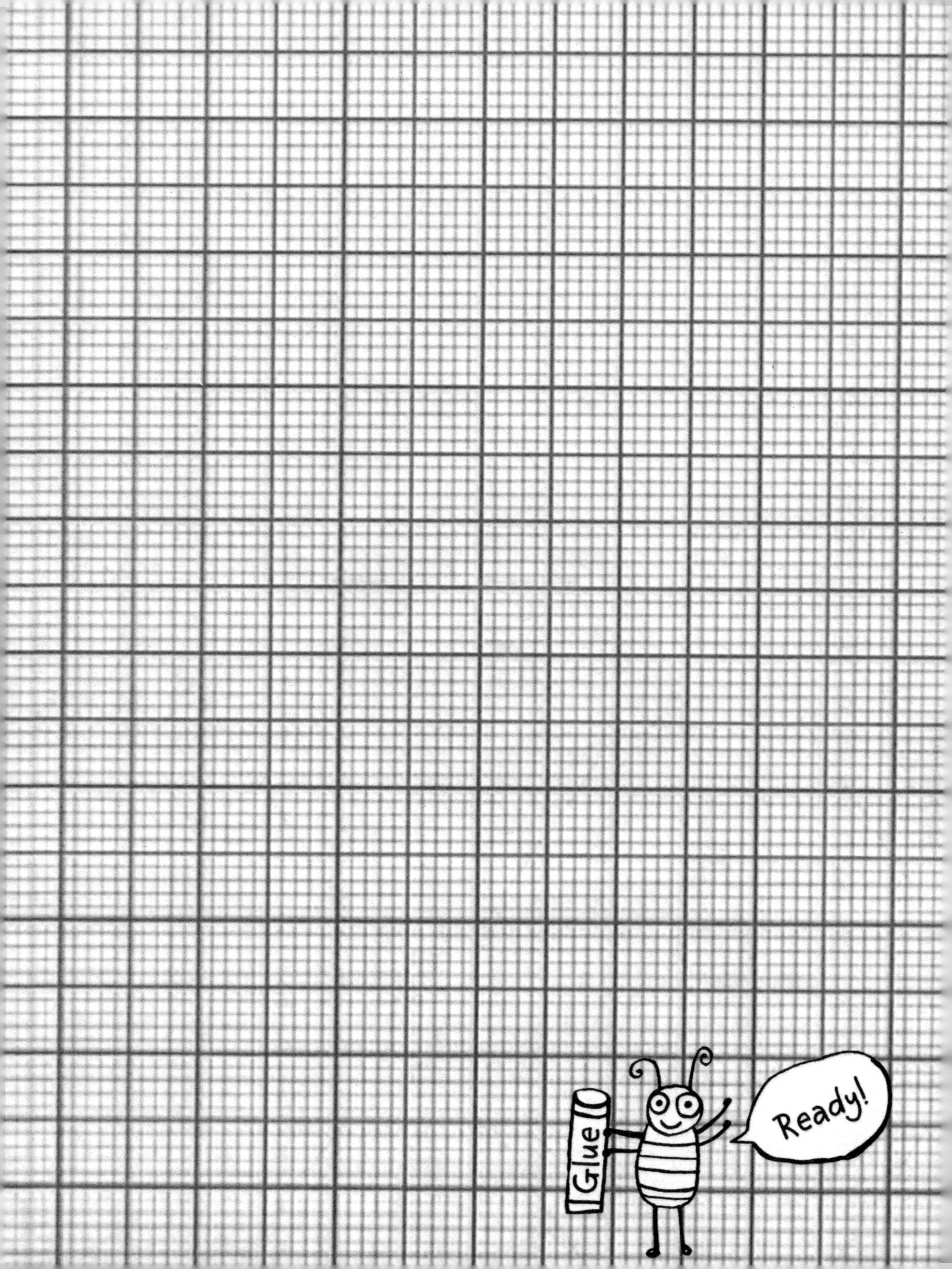
Glue
Ready!

JUST ADD FABU

OUS COLOURS!

# Very HEAVY Triangle

Draw what is holding it up.

# Draw Your Teachers

Mr Fullerman and his BEADY EYES

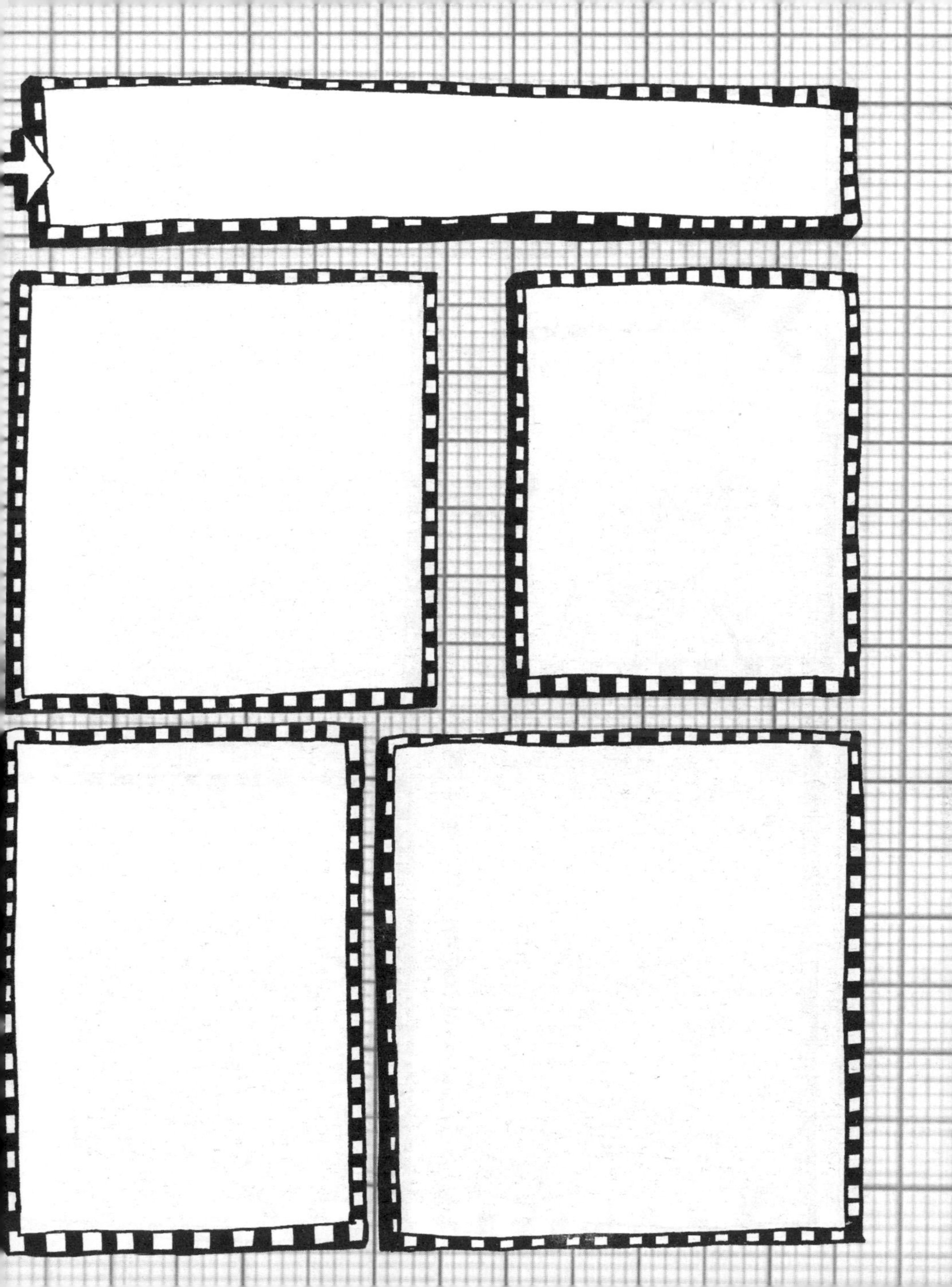

Pretend chalkboard for top doodles and notes
Use a white pen or pencil to fill this page.
Doodle not.

Doodle on this page
to make you look busy
Paint

Test your pens out here.

Pens at the ready!

# Fill

this page with
lots of swirls.

MY
TOP
5
PETS
1. Cute dog
What about me?
2. Big dog
4. Perky dog
5. Fluffy dog
3. Sausage dog

Draw pictures of
YOUR TOP 5 PETS.
TOP
5
1
2
3
4
5

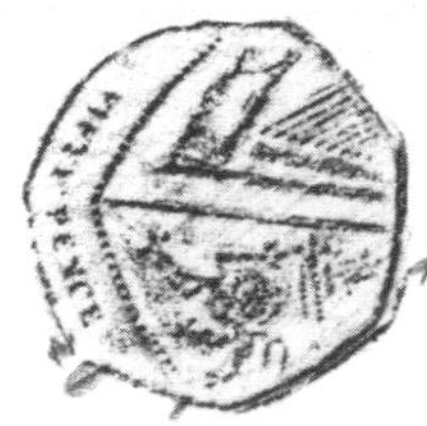


**FILL these** pages
with rubbings from coins
or flat interesting objects.
Pop the coin under the page
and use the side of a
pencil to rub
over the top.

Very funny

SPRING
Trees, Shoes and
Tiny Warblers

Here's my face when Mr Fullerman says...

**There's been a change of plan. It's such a beautiful SPRING DAY, I'd like to do a different lesson and take you all outside.**

Which sounds EXCITING!

Looking around, I'm not the only one who's happy about the change of plan.

**"We're going to be discovering the WONDER of plants and incredible wildlife that's all around us."**

This lesson is getting BETTER and BETTER. Sounds like we're going on a TRIP!

"SIR, are you taking us to a **wildlife park?"**

Florence asks.

"Can we feed the animals? Do they like cheese?" Norman wants to know.

Mr Fullerman gives him one of his LOOKS (which means ... NO).

**"It's SO much better than that.**

**We're going outside to ...**

## the school grounds!

Mr Fullerman tries to make it sound good, but we all know a **wildlife park** is MUCH better than the school grounds.

Norman expresses his feelings loudly. –

"AAAAAAAAAwwwwwwwwwwwwwwwwwwwwwwwwwwwwwwww!"

**You'd be SURPRISED by the EXCITING wildlife and plants that are RIGHT in front of you.**

**There's probably an INCREDIBLE insect that's flying past *this* window right NOW.**

Everyone turns to look out of the window...

Caretaker Stan is walking past. He's not sure why we're staring at him – so he WAVES.

We wave back.

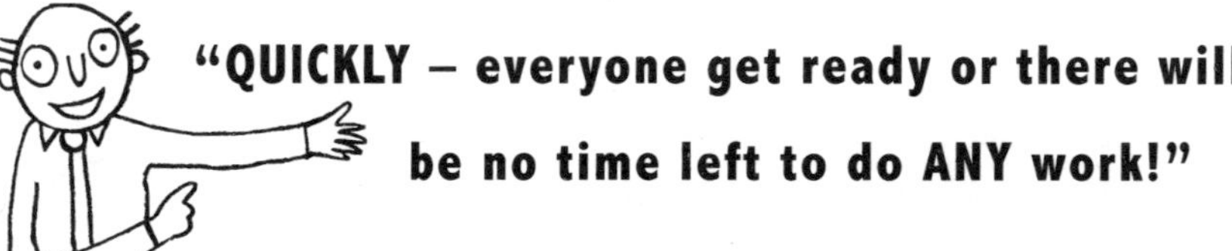

**"QUICKLY – everyone get ready or there will be no time left to do ANY work!"**

Mr Fullerman says, trying to hurry us all up.

Some kids take that as a challenge to move even ...
SLOWER.

(Mr Fullerman is WISE to this trick.)

**"Solid, WHY are you holding a chair?"** Mr Fullerman asks.

"To sit on outside, sir."

(Good thinking, Solid.)

Everyone starts picking up chairs because this is a very good idea.

**"No chairs! Just a pen, paper and something to REST ON...**

**Not a TABLE, Brad,"** Mr Fullerman says.

He's sighing a lot now.

We start to line up and then follow Mr Fullerman down the corridor.

For some reason, Norman keeps jumping up and down.

I can see Mrs Mumble walking towards us. She's SMILING at first, but the closer she gets, the more worried she looks.

"Did I miss a fire alarm, Mr Fullerman?"

**"No, Mrs Mumble – it's just such a LOVELY SPRING day that we're going outside to do our work and study the interesting plants and LOCAL wildlife on the school grounds."**

Mrs Mumble seems pleased about that.

"HOW fantastic! I heard on the radio this morning that there's been sightings of a VERY RARE and beautiful bird called a Tiny Golden Warbler," she tells us.

"It hasn't been seen in OAKFIELD TOWN for over **TWENTY YEARS** and it's suddenly **BACK**."

Mr Fullerman says.

"Hands up if you've ever seen a picture of a Tiny Golden Warbler before,"

Mrs Mumble asks us hopefully.

Norman puts his hand up quickly.

Wonderful!
Do tell everyone what's SO special about the bird, Norman.

"I just need the TOILET PLEASE."

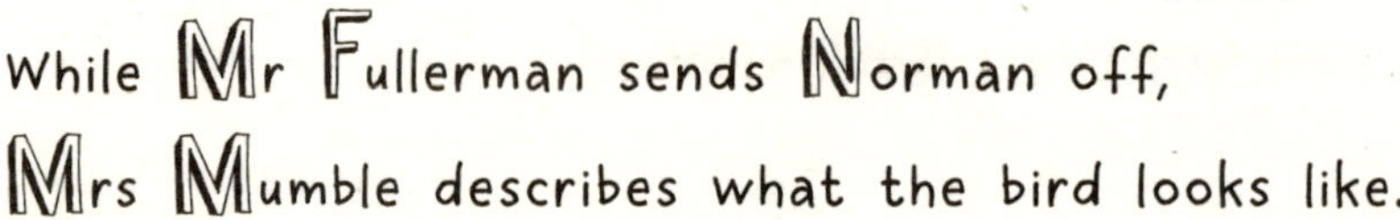

While Mr Fullerman sends Norman off,

Mrs Mumble describes what the bird looks like.

It's very small BUT with **GLORIOUS** bright yellow feathers on its head that look like a little crown. And if you're **LUCKY** enough to see one – it's a magical moment. So **KEEP** a **LOOK-OUT** as you never know. Imagine the **RARE** bird coming to our school! I'd put it in the school newsletter for sure!

**"We'll try our best, Mrs Mumble. Won't we, class?"** Mr Fullerman says.

We sort of reply "YES" but it doesn't sound like anyone is *that* excited about a bird.

(If we were going to a **wildlife park** that might be different.)

"I'll probably SPOT the bird as I've got VERY good EYESIGHT," Marcus tells me.

"LOOK – there it is!"

I point to the window again.

"WHERE? LET ME SEE!"

Marcus shouts.

"Made you look..." I LAUGH.

"You'll scare it away if you talk THAT LOUDLY, Marcus!" AMY tells him.

"I won't – I knew Tom was only joking," Marcus says.

(He didn't.)

Mr Fullerman heads outside and STOPS at a large plant pot and waits for us to catch up.

There are a few of these pots in the school grounds that have nice flowers and plants in.

They used to have pebbles too, but when the stone-collection CRAZE started, kids kept taking them and now there's none left.

**"Gather round, EVERYONE. OK – does anyone know what THIS type of plant is called?"** Mr Fullerman wants to know.

I say, and everyone LAUGHS.

**"I don't think it's DEAD, Tom. If you look CLOSELY, you'll see the tiny buds about to BURST into life on this CAMELLIA plant."**

We all move forward.

"It still looks ... dead, sir," AMY says.

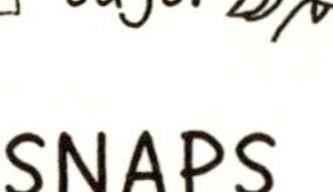

Then Mr Fullerman accidentally SNAPS a branch OFF (because it's dead).

**"OH! You might be right. Shall we see what's in the SOIL instead? There's always plenty of bugs and creatures to be found if you dig down a little deeper—"** he tells us, and starts to move the soil with the branch.

## "What have we got HERE?"

Mr Fullerman finds something and holds up ...

a bottle top.

**"THIS should be in the BIN."**

Then Pansy find another one.

"Hey, sir, I've found a RED bottle top!"

"I've got a BLUE one!" Leroy adds.

"Here's a GREEN one – maybe that's why the plant died?" Marcus suggests.

"We should start collecting bottle tops instead of STONES. They make excellent badges too," I point out, and everyone starts searching for MORE bottle tops.

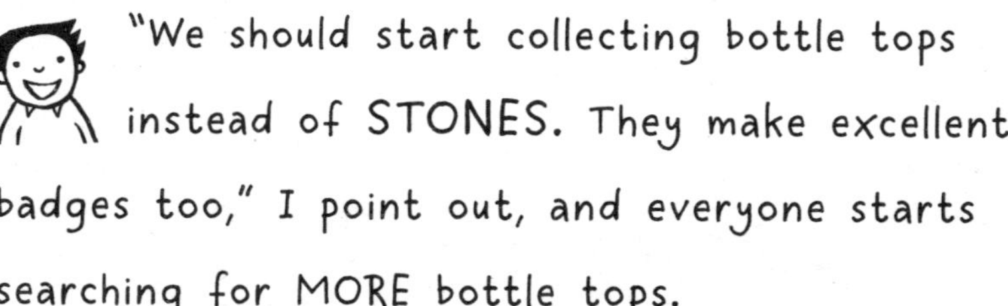

**"No one should be putting bottle tops IN the PLANT POTS. Come along – follow me over to that BIG TREE. I'll tell you some interesting FACTS about leaves."**

(As Mr Fullerman heads off, I find a red bottle top.)

I'm so busy looking at my bottle top I don't notice that everyone's left me. Mr Fullerman is now standing under the BIG TREE trying to get the class EXCITED about leaves.

(I'm not sure THIS is the lesson Mr Fullerman was planning.)

**"This is a HORNBEAM tree that's been in the school grounds for a LONG time – it's quite old."**

"Is it as old as you, sir?" Solid asks.

**"OLDER,"** he says, and Solid goes "Ooohhhhh..." like he's shocked.

**"This is a DECIDUOUS tree.**

**Does anyone know what that means?"**

"It's a TREE ... that's DANGEROUS.

SIR ... an ANT'S crawled up my leg!"

Norman says while wiggling his leg around.

Julia Morton puts up her hand to tell us,

"Trees CAN be dangerous.

I fell out of a tree and broke my arm, sir."

"I've done that,"

Norman adds.

(So have I - but it was mostly the doughnut's fault.*)

**"It's not dangerous – it means the leaves fall OFF the branches in the autumn,"**

Mr Fullerman explains ... slowly.

* See my book *Random Acts of Fun.*

We're listening to Mr Fullerman talking about **"the shape of the LEAVES..."** when a SHOE goes flying through the air and gets STUCK in the branches.
**Who did that?**
he shouts.
It's not hard to guess as Brad's only wearing one shoe and a sock.

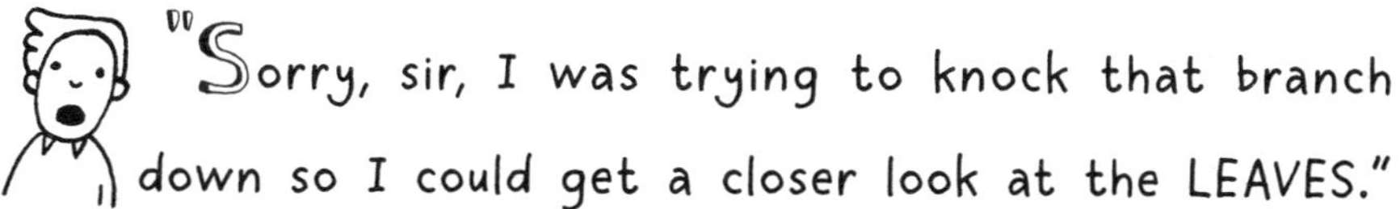

"Sorry, sir, I was trying to knock that branch down so I could get a closer look at the LEAVES."

**"Of course you were, Brad – why else would you THROW your shoe into the tree?"**

Mr Fullerman sounds fed up.

We watch as he tries to REACH UP and grab it – but he's too short.

Then Mr Fullerman SHAKES the tree.

But that doesn't work either.

Next, he throws his CLIPBOARD right into the branches ... where it stays.

"Sir, we could all throw our shoes up together – that might work,"

I suggest.

**"No,"** Mr Fullerman tells us.

**"I'm going to get a BALL. Everyone carry on filling in your worksheets."**

The first thing Brad does is throw his other shoe...

And that gets stuck as well.

"Aww - now I've got no shoes," Brad complains.

"Mr Fullerman told you not to," Marcus reminds him.

I sit down on the grass and start to answer the questions.

1. DESCRIBE SOME OF THE PLANTS YOU'VE SEEN:

*Mostly dead twigs.*

2. WHAT DID YOU FIND IN THE SOIL?

*A nice collection of different-coloured BOTTLE TOPS!*

Mr Fullerman returns with a tennis ball.

**"Keep clear, everyone,"** he says.

The rest of the class sit on the grass and enjoy watching Mr Fullerman do underarm throws to knock the shoes and clipboard out of the tree.

**"This won't take long,"** he tells us.

(This is not true.)

He's still throwing the ball when AMY says,

"Sir, Mrs Mumble is waving at us from the school office."

"I think she's trying to get your attention, sir," AMY lets him know.

Mrs Mumble's not just WAVING.

She's leaping around and looks very HAPPY!

**"She's probably wondering why I'm throwing the ball into the tree,"** he tells us.

**"It's OK, Mrs Mumble – I'm just trying to get my clipboard down!"**

Mr Fullerman calls back, and gives her the THUMBS UP.

**"I'll explain LATER, Mrs Mumble!"**

**"Brad, I'll ask Caretaker Stan if he can get your shoe down now,"** he adds.

"My SHOES, sir – they've both got stuck," Brad tells him

Mr Fullerman sighs.

I haven't seen many CREATURES or bugs but it's lovely being in the SUNSHINE, drawing the tree.

Marcus isn't happy though – he sat on a wet patch of grass and now he's complaining.

Back in the classroom, Mrs Mumble is THERE waiting for us.

**"Hello, Mrs Mumble – is everything OK?"**

Mr Fullerman asks, as this is UNUSUAL.

She's still HAPPY and ever so ☆EXCITED☆ to tell us:

"Wasn't that the MOST wonderful sight? I couldn't believe MY EYES!"

**"I was trying to get my clipboard down from the tree – and Brad's shoe,"** Mr Fullerman explains.

"My SHOES, sir, and now my socks are wet," Brad adds.

"And I've got a wet patch too," Marcus grumbles.

"Didn't you see the Tiny Golden Warbler? It was IN the TREE and flying around you!

That RARE special bird was HERE IN OAKFIELD SCHOOL! You did see it, didn't you, Mr Fullerman? ANYone?" Mrs Mumble asks us.

Norman puts up his hand.

**"Did you see it, NORMAN?"**

Mr Fullerman asks.

"No, sir, I just need the toilet."

Mr Fullerman sighs loudly again.

**"It's nearly breaktime, Norman, you can wait. I can't believe we MISSED the RARE bird, Mrs Mumble. That's so disappointing."**

"And I thought your class were busy drawing the tiny bird up in the tree," Mrs Mumble tells him.

While Mr Fullerman and Mrs Mumble chat about missing out on seeing the Tiny Golden Warbler, Norman walks over to the window and says...

"Hey, look at that!"

We look out of the window.

And THERE on the GRASS is ... the Tiny Golden Warbler. It really is BRIGHT YELLOW with a crown of feathers on its head.

"Mr Fullerman!
Mr Fullerman!

It's the bird!"

Marcus calls out SO LOUDLY the bird hears him and flies OFF.

**"Where is it?"** Mr Fullerman asks.

"You were too slow, sir," Marcus says.

"You were too LOUD, Marcus," AMY reminds him.

Then I say, "Don't worry, sir, it'll come back – in twenty years."

And Mr Fullerman smiles, then sighs.

## The GOOD NEWS is...

Mr Fullerman and everyone else who missed out on seeing the RARE bird get to read all about it in the **SPECIAL EDITION** of the **OAKFIELD SCHOOL NEWSLETTER** that Mrs Mumble has put together.

Our class has an excellent **NATURE table display** too. There's TREE drawings, different-shaped leaves, dead twigs, bottle tops and, best of all, pictures of the Tiny Golden Warbler. And I even made my bottle top into a very nice badge. Lessons outside in spring are the best.

# SPACE FOR YOUR OWN STORY

# DRAW PICTURES to GO with YOUR STORY

Bring these plants BACK to life.

I was hungry!
The whole plant?

# MAKE a bird GAME

## You can trace this BIRD or draw your own.

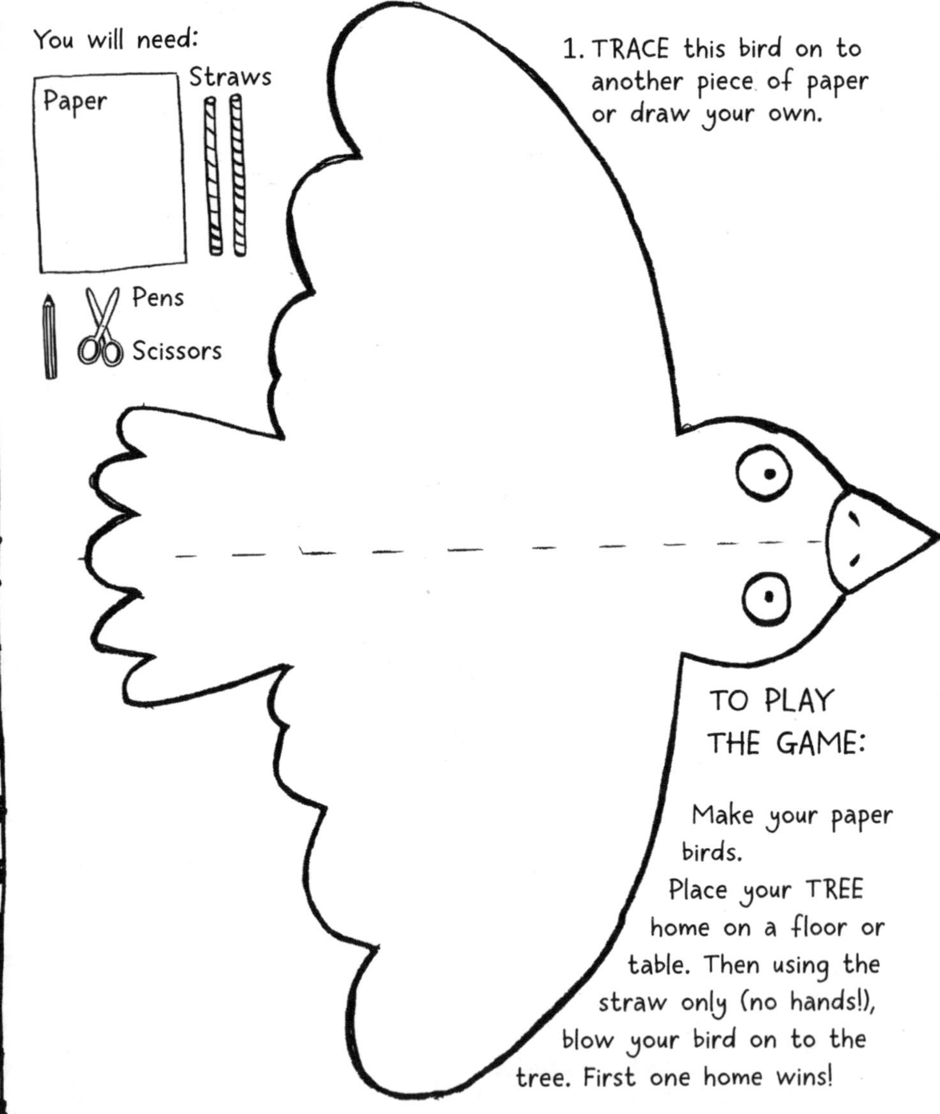

You will need:

Paper

Straws

Pens

Scissors

1. TRACE this bird on to another piece of paper or draw your own.

TO PLAY THE GAME:

Make your paper birds. Place your TREE home on a floor or table. Then using the straw only (no hands!), blow your bird on to the tree. First one home wins!

2. Once you've drawn your bird, colour it in and fold it in half.

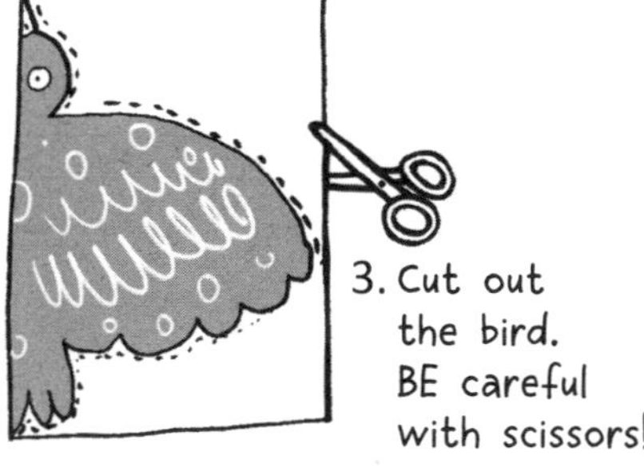

3. Cut out the bird. BE careful with scissors!

4. Your bird's ready!

5. Then draw a tree for its HOME on another piece of paper. Place it on the floor or on a table.

Then get ready...

Get set...

GO!

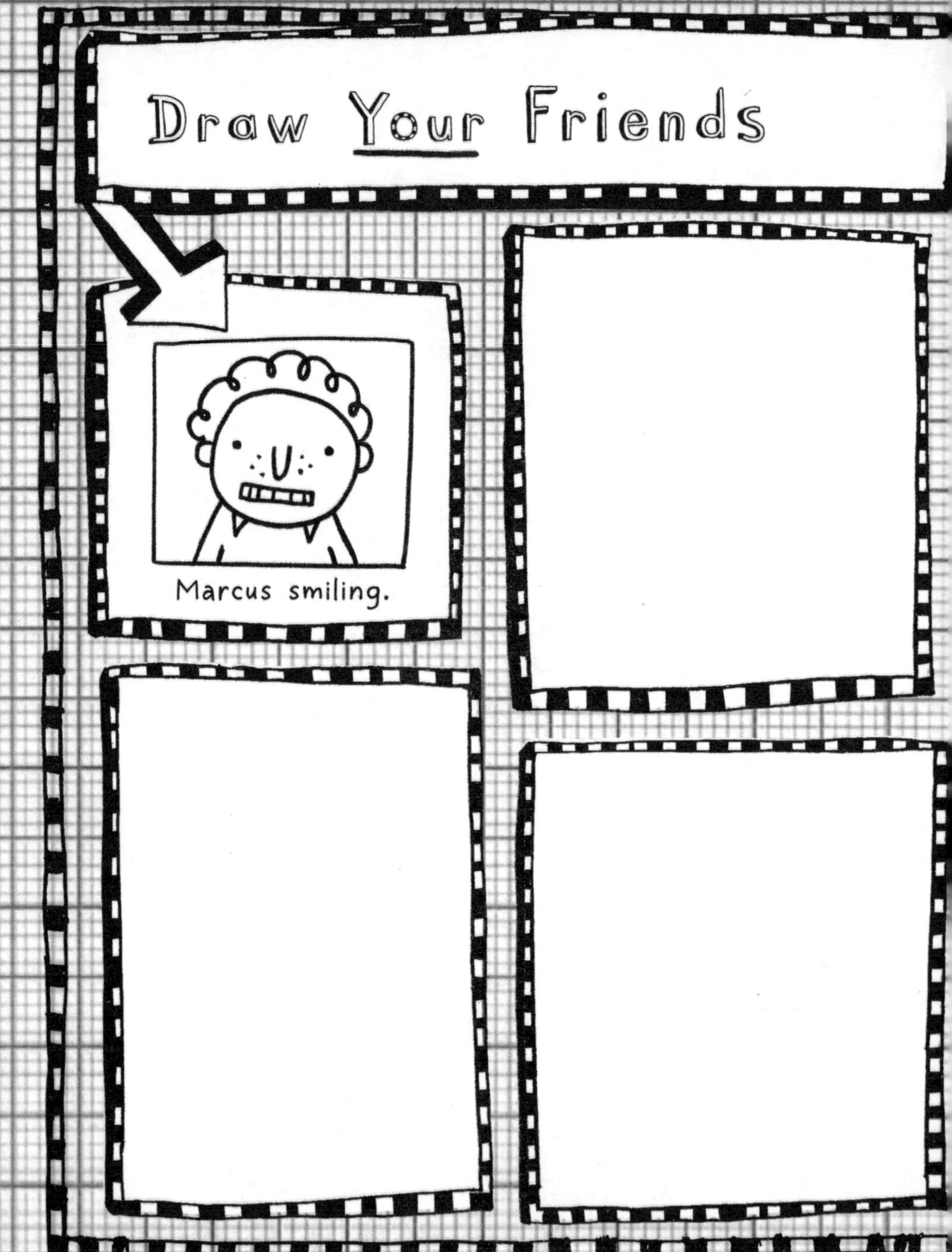
Draw Your Friends
Marcus smiling.

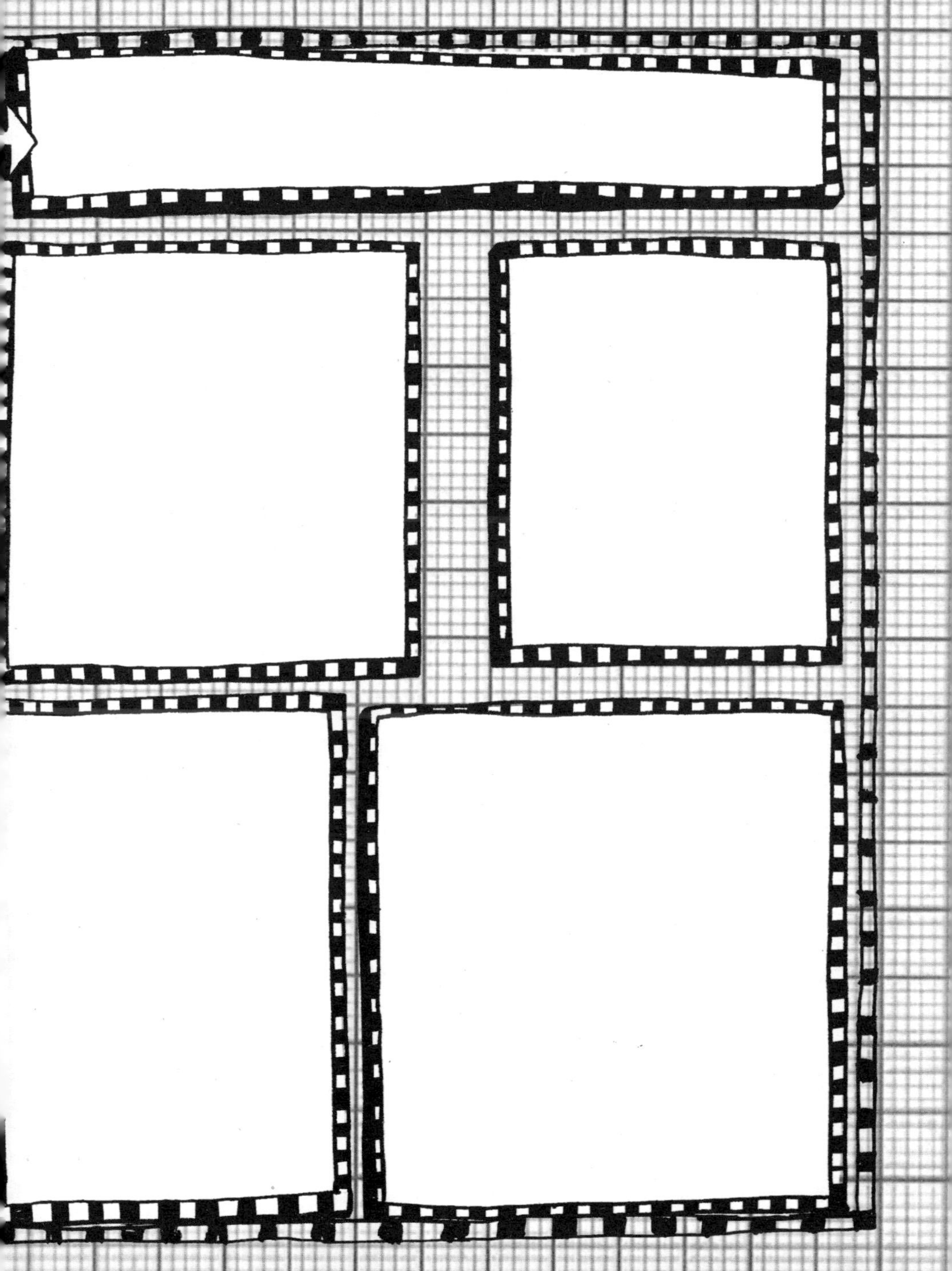

What's the sound under ground?

tom tom

TOM tOM TOM TOM

Tom

T

TOM TOM TOM

Tom

TOM TOM TOM TOM TOM Tom

Tom Tom TOM Tom TOM Tom TOM

Tom Tom TOM Tom Tom tom

tom TOM tom Tom Tom Tom Tom tom

Tom Tom Tom Tom Tom Tom tom

tom Tom Tom Tom Tom Tom Tom TOM TOM tom

Tom Tom Tom Tom TOM

So many Toms.

TOM Tom Tom TOM

Tom Tom Tom

Tom Tom tom

Tom Tom tom TOM TOM Tom Tom tom

TOM Tom tom Tom

WRITE your NAME LOADS OF DIFFERENT WAYS and FILL THE PAGE.

ADD MORE WIGGLY LINES.

FILL
these circles
with YOUR
FAVOURITE
WORDS.
FUN

JUST ADD

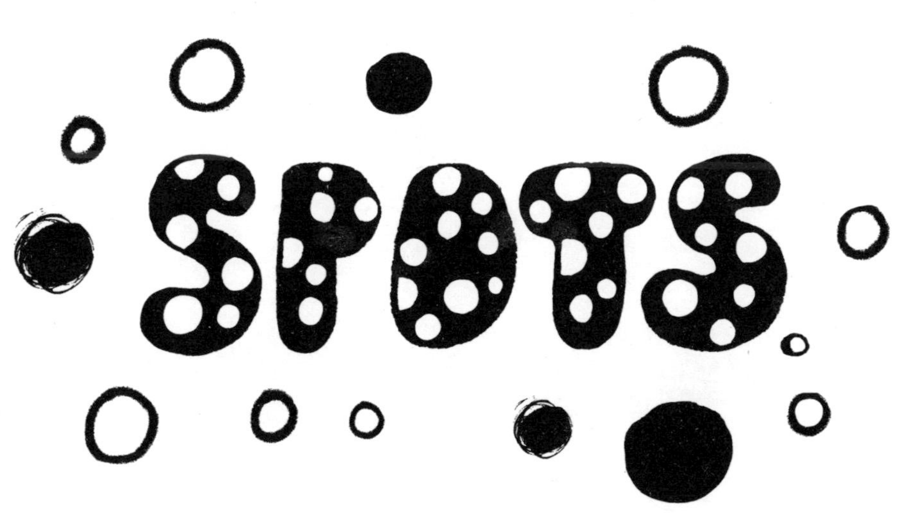
SPOTS

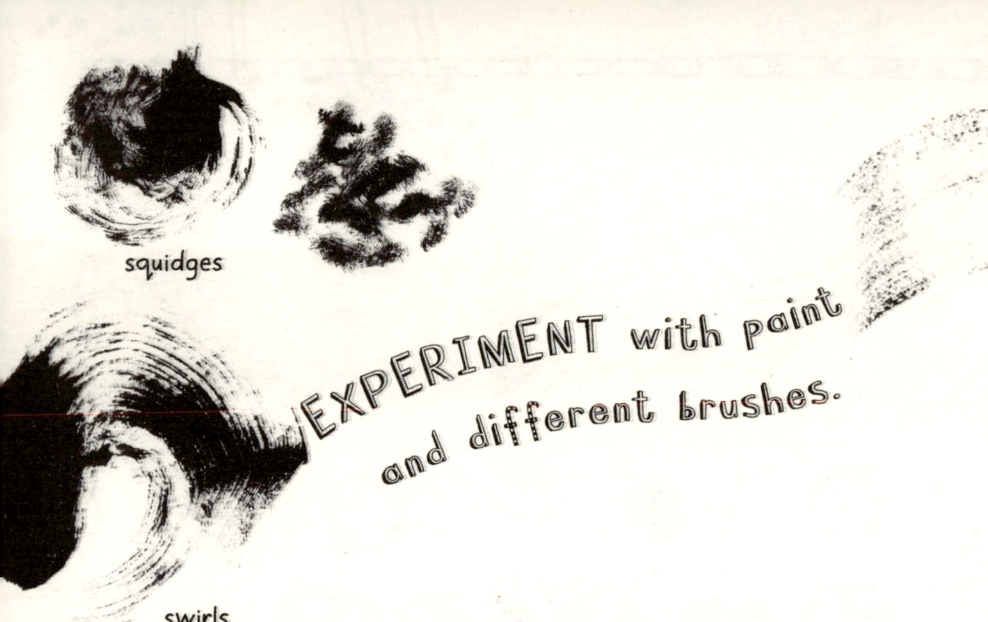
squidges
swirls
EXPERIMENT with paint
and different brushes.

FRee
Go wild!

STYLE

FIND THE FOUR-LEAF CLOVERS, COLOUR THEM IN AND ADD MORE, MORE, MORE!

I will
FIND them
ALL!

You will need:

- Air-drying clay
- Pens
- Paint to decorate

1. Shape your clay into a rectangle. Make it deep enough to hold the pens.

2. Use water to smooth the edges with your fingers.

3. Then take the END of the pen you want to put in the holder. →

Gently push it into the clay to make a hole.

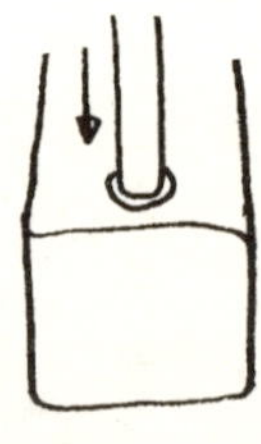

4. Space the holes along the rectangle. If it moves out of shape – pat it back into a rectangle and re-do the hole.

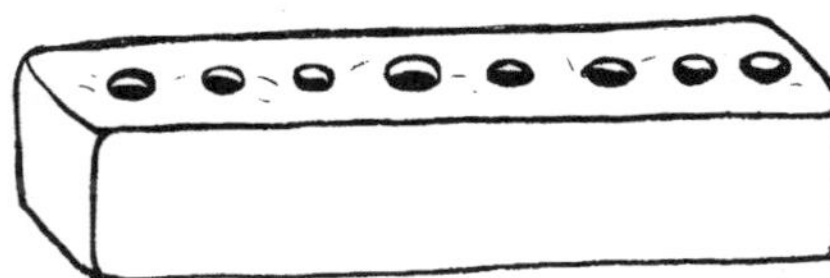

Let it dry completely. Be patient!

5. Decorate with paint, pens, or both. Let it dry again.

6. Put your pens in your new pen holder!

That's not me...

SUMMER
What ice cream?

I'm sitting in the garden when I hear MUSIC.

Not just any old MUSIC.

It's the SOUND of the ICE-CREAM VAN.

I could do with a lolly or an ice cream as it's a really HOT day (and I like ice cream).

I run into the house as *FAST* as I can because the ice-cream van doesn't hang around. You have to be *QUICK*.

Dad's on the phone and can't talk. I let him know this is an **EMERGENCY** and act out

"Ice cream from the ice-cream van" so he knows what I'm asking.

Go and ask your mum...

he tells me, and points upstairs.

I go and find her *FAST.*

(The music keeps playing, which means the van is still there, but for how long?)

3 mins gone.

There's NO time to waste.

Mum's in the bathroom.

So I KNOCK LOUDLY and call out:

Mum! Mum!
The ice-cream van's here!
Can we get ice cream?

I don't know where Delia is, and Dad's still on the phone.

This is NOT ideal, but I can't waste any more time.

"I'll GIVE DELIA the MONEY back and I'll have a 99*..."

Now Mum wants an ice cream too.

The quickest way to find Delia is to SHOUT...

* A 99 is a type of ice cream in a cone with a chocolate flake.

Delia doesn't answer.

I **BARGE** into her room but she's not there either. "**DELIA!**" I call out.

Then I RUN BACK downstairs, where I FIND her sitting in the NEW swivel chair with her headphones on. She looks very relaxed until I SPIN her to get her attention.

"**DELIA!** Mum said you can come with me to BUY ICE CREAM from the ICE-CREAM VAN - QUICKLY!"

**"STOP SPINNING ME, TOM!"**

(At least she's listening now...)

The ice-cream van will leave if we don't go...

"Calm down, Tom - it's only ice cream."

"It's **NOT** just ice cream. It's 99's with flakes and sprinkles!"

(That gets Delia moving - everyone likes 99's.)

Outside, I can **SEE** the van is parked at the end of our road - **AND** there's no queue.

Which is **BRILLIANT!**

As we get closer ...

the van suddenly ...

**DRIVES OFF!**

NO! Come back!

Oh dear! Never mind, Tom.

This is a **DISASTER!** It doesn't even have its music on – which means it's NOT going to stop again. I watch the van disappear ... sadly.

Delia doesn't seem that bothered.

"<u>You</u> were <u>SO</u> slow – we missed the ice-cream van. It's gone now."

"Don't blame me. You shouldn't have spent so much time spinning me in the chair!" Delia says.

It's a long slow walk home for me... ☹

All the time I'm getting hotter. If ONLY I had something to cool me down, like an ice cream ... or an ice lolly.

Delia gets home before me, because I keep hoping the van will SUDDENLY come back and I'm listening out for the music, but there's nothing.

I might as well go and SIT in the NEW chair and have a SPIN.

This will CHEER me up and take my mind off missing out on a 99 ice cream – a bit.

BUT I can't even do **THAT!** Delia's sitting in the chair and looking all comfortable and **SMUG.**

THEN I notice...

She's ONLY EATING AN ICE LOLLY!

"HEY, WHERE DID YOU GET THAT FROM?"

I want to know.

"I MADE THEM YESTERDAY - do you want one?" Delia says unexpectedly, and hands ME a lolly.

"Have you licked it?" I check, because it's the sort of thing I'd do.

"No, Tom. Don't take it then," she says.

"I'll have it - thanks, Delia."

I taste the lolly carefully, just in case.

"What do you think?" Delia wants to know.

"It's OK - not as good as a 99, but not bad," I tell her. (Which is TRUE.)

"Can I sit in the chair now?"

"No, and don't spin me," she says, which is a mistake.

(Of course I'm going to spin her.)

# SPACE FOR YOUR OWN STORY

# DRAW PICTURES to GO with YOUR STORY

DRAW what Delia is looking at in her glasses.

DRAW a CLOSE-UP of someone you know with glasses.

# Make Fruit-Juice Lollies

You will need:

- Ice-cube tray or lolly mould
- Straws or wooden sticks
- Fruit juice
- A jug (if you have one)

1. Use a lolly mould or make tiny lollies with an ice-cube tray. Pour the fruit juice into the mould or tray.
Use a jug if it's easier.

2. Pop in the freezer until almost frozen. (Check it after an hour or so.) Then take them out and pop the stick or straw into the juice. Put back in the freezer until fully frozen.

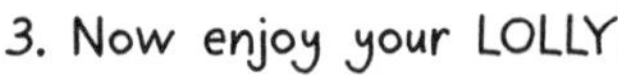

3. Now enjoy your LOLLY!

Colour this lolly

Draw Your Favourite Animals

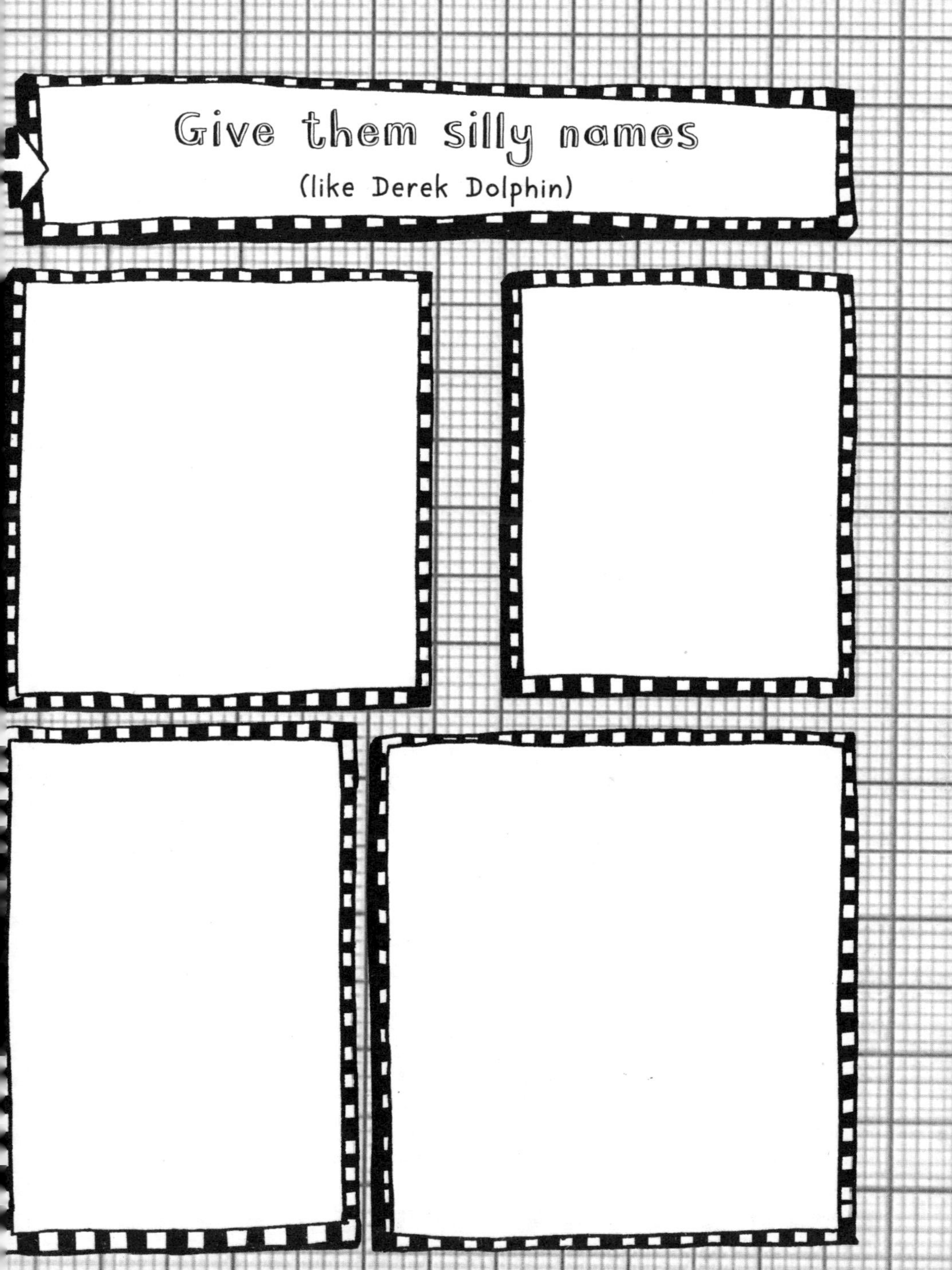
Give them silly names
(like Derek Dolphin)

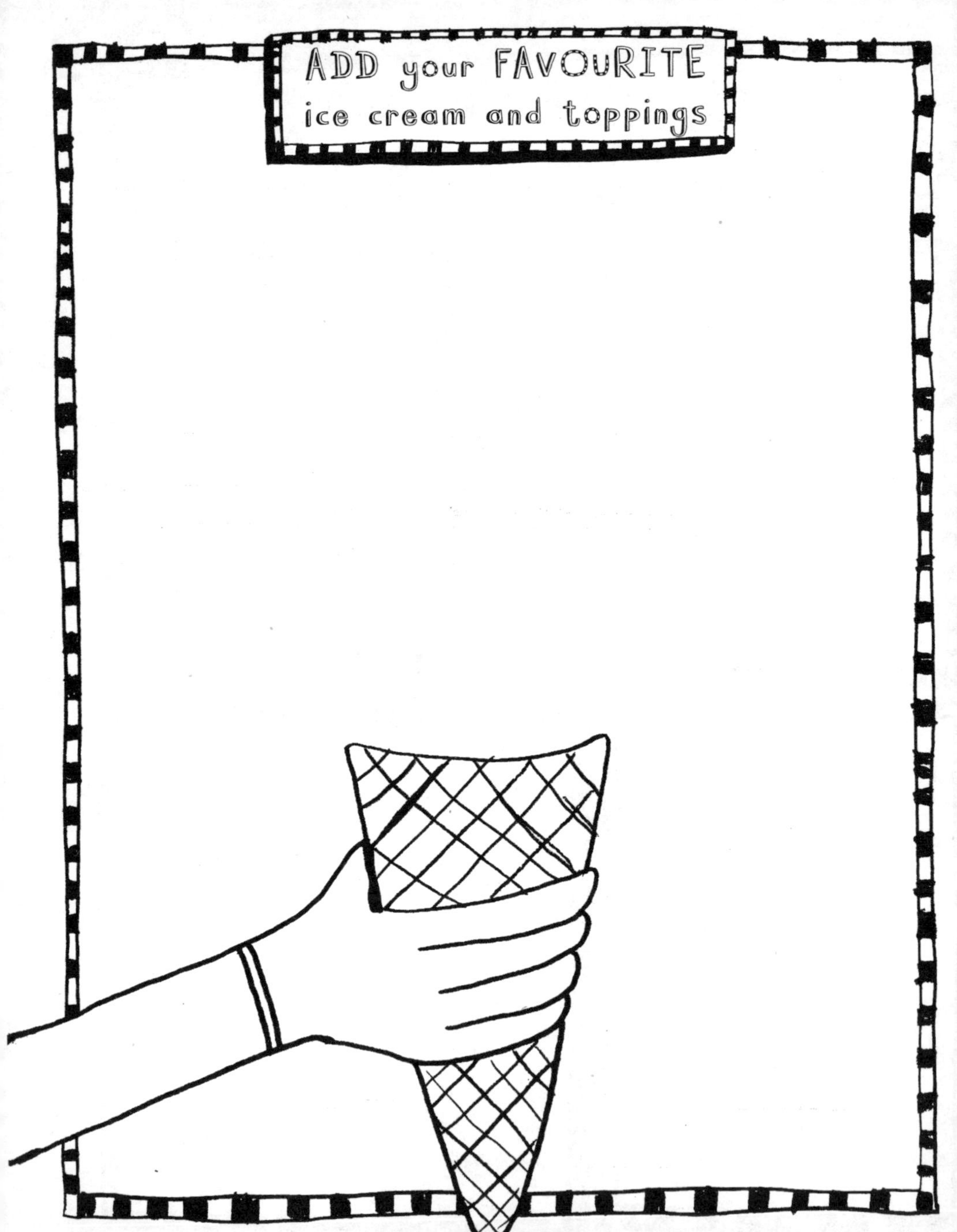
ADD your FAVOURITE
ice cream and toppings

WHAT giant ice cream over my head?

IT'S RAINING cats, dogs
and so many other things too.

Draw what else is raining.

MONSTER
DOODLE
Colour
ME

You will need:
An old T-shirt 

A4 paper

Fabric pens or paint

Pencil

Black pen

Rubber

1. This is a GREAT way to make an OLD tee look AMAZING again! Take your T-shirt and cover up a stain or add doodles to the old design.

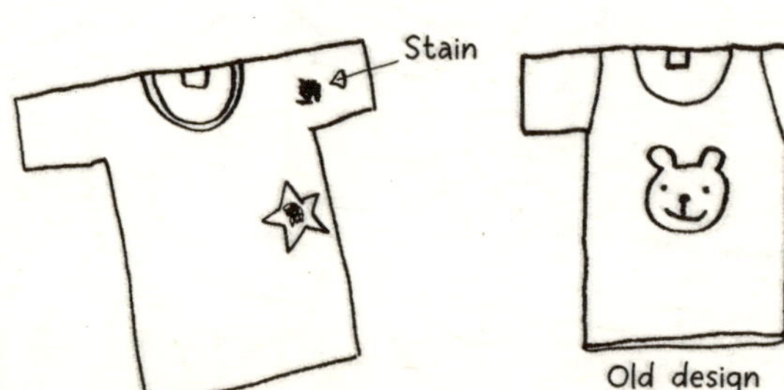

New design

2.

Draw your design in black pen on A4 paper.

3.

Next, slip it inside your T-shirt.

4.

Now use your fabric pens or paint to draw your design on to your T-shirt.

Trace this T-shirt and use it to work out your design.

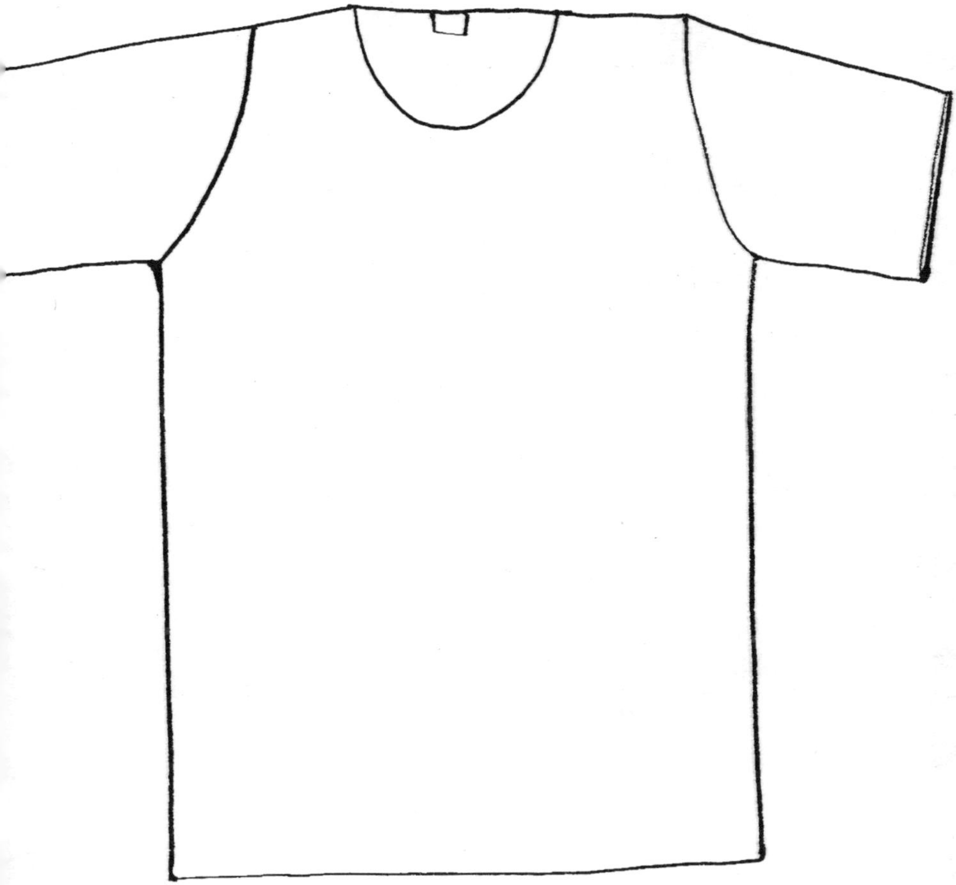

5. Follow the FABRIC pens or paint instructions to FIX the design. Do get a grown-up to help you. Then wear your T-shirt and tell EVERYONE YOU designed it!

TOM'S
TOP
5
BOOKS
WHAT
MONSTERS?

What are YOUR
TOP books?
TOP
5
1
2
3
4
5

# Noughts and Crosses

Take turns to put an O or an X in the spaces. The first one to make a line either across or diagonally wins.

I win!

# HOW TO PLAY BOXES

Take turns to draw lines connecting the dots to make boxes. The person who finishes the box CLAIMS it by putting their initial inside (or symbol). You have to take a turn, even if it means the other person will take the box. The winner has the most boxes when all the squares are completed.

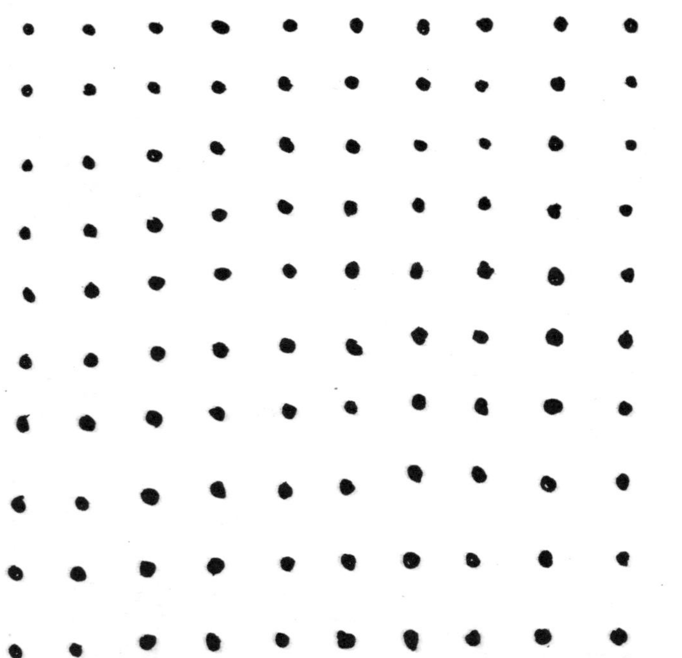

What are the monsters' hopes and dreams?

What are YOUR
hopes and dreams?

Colour in the squares
(if you have a spare ten hours...)

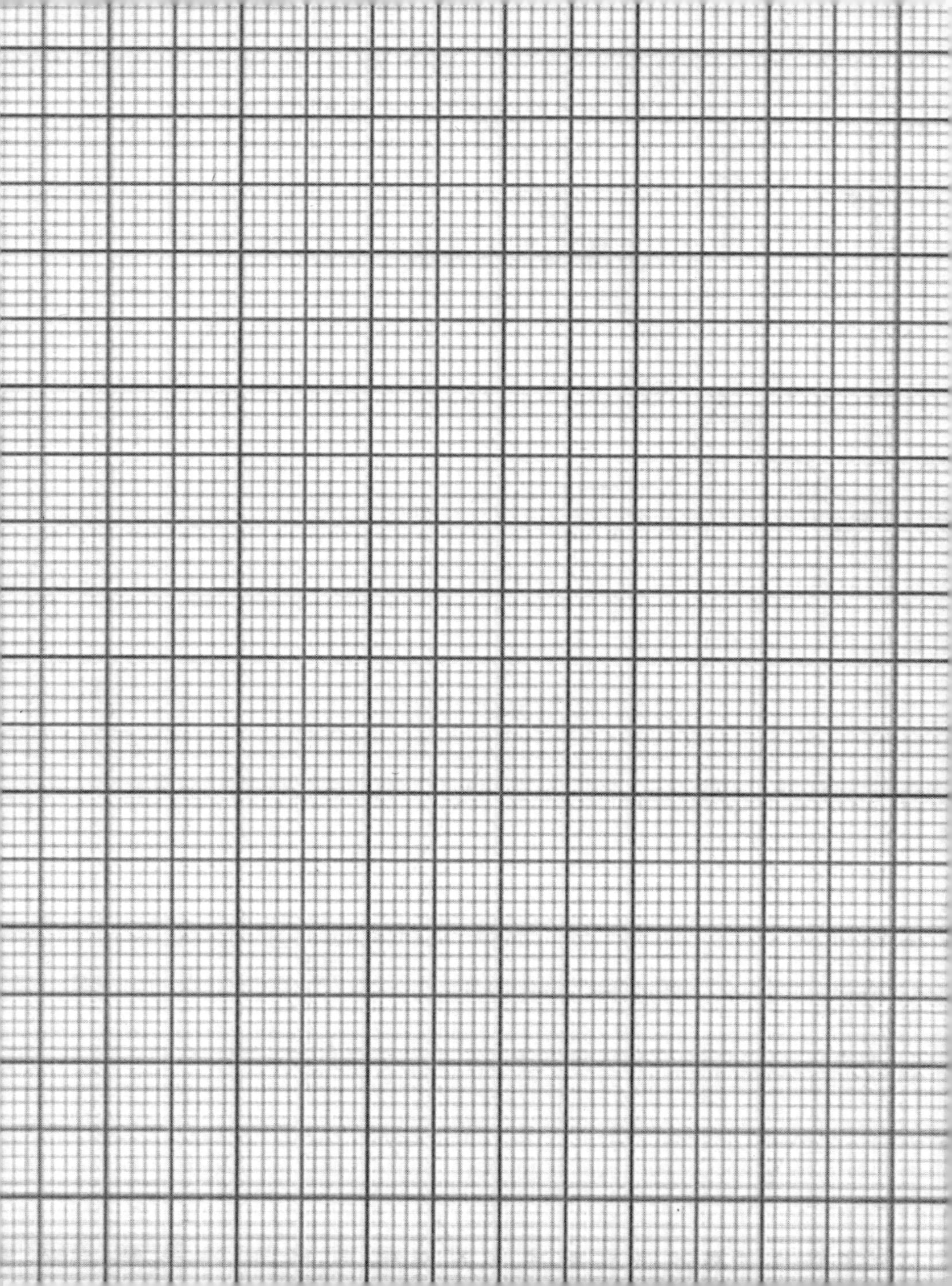

Get your friends to sign HERE

# EXTREME CLOSE-UP OF...

Dear Marcus,
STOP being a nosy parker and reading over my shoulder. This is MY book where I can write and draw anything I want to - like THIS!

AUTUMN
A short story
about leaves

whoopee
AGH!
YiPee
Sigh

BIN
Leaf!
Leaf collection
Home
HI!

DRAW YOUR OWN COMIC SPREAD

# SPACE FOR YOUR OWN STORY

DRAW PICTURES to GO with YOUR STORY

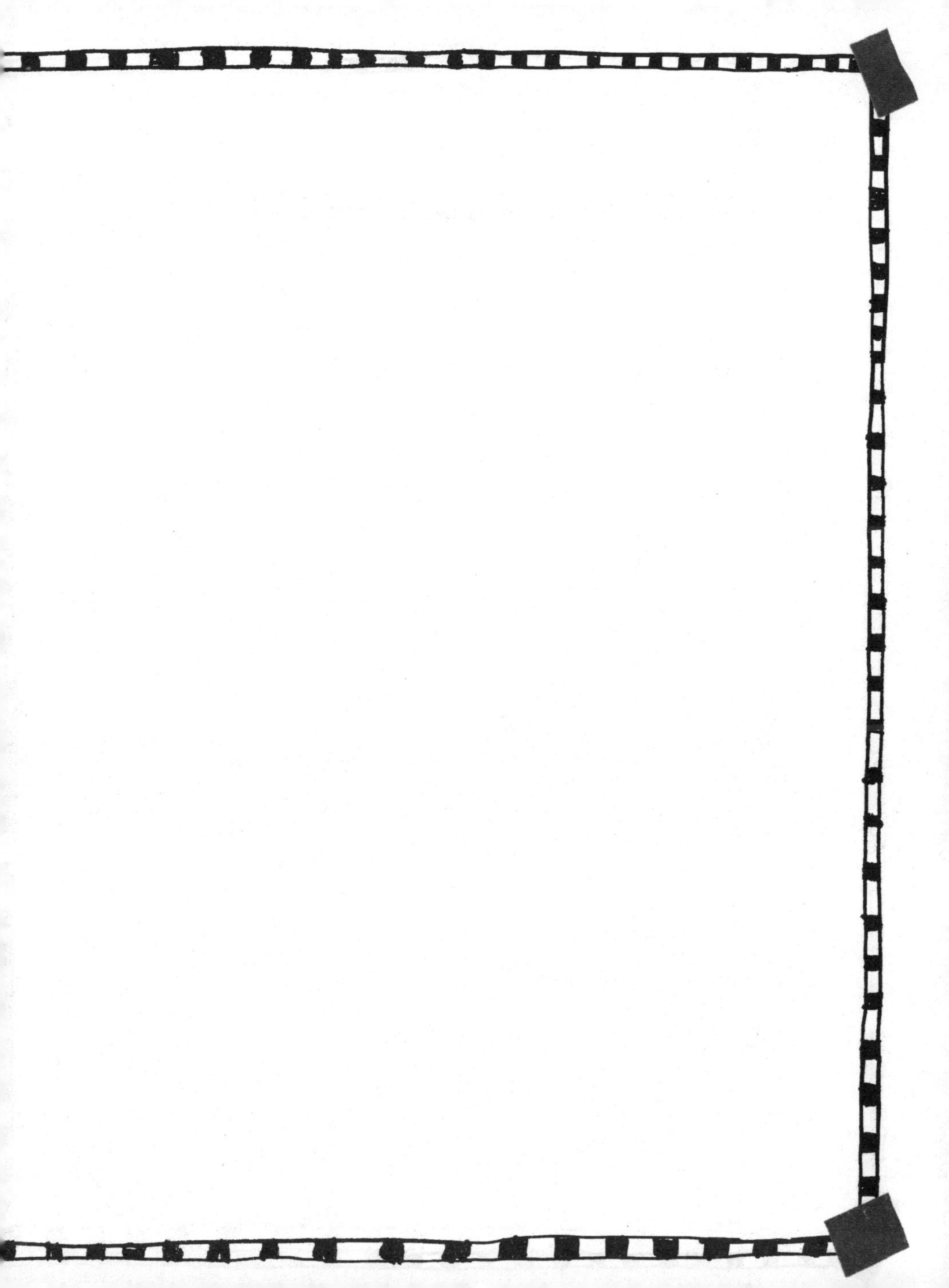

STICK INTERESTING LEAVES ON THESE PAGES.

ExPress
yourself!

I am.

# PAPER-CHAIN GHOSTS

You will need: Thin A4 paper, scissors, glue, black pen.

Take a sheet of A4 paper, fold it longways in half and carefully cut it along the fold.

Then glue the two halves together.

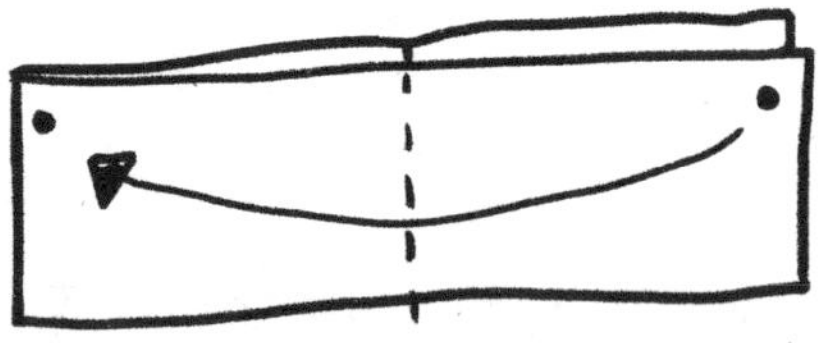

Fold the long paper in half.
Then fold in half again,
and again
and again.

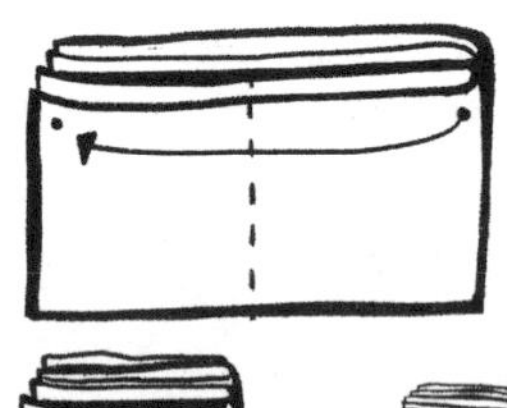

Folded side of the paper

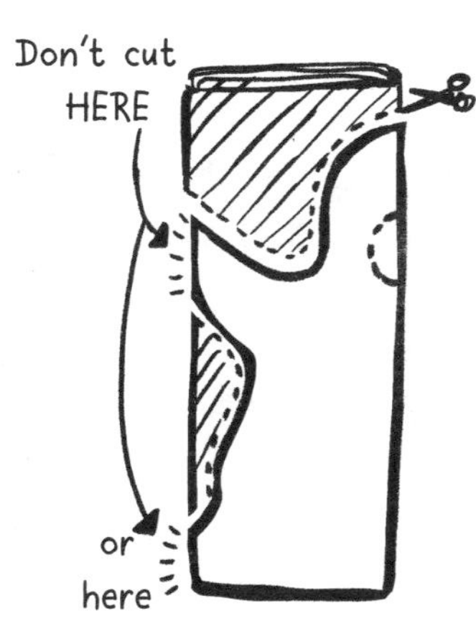


Draw half a ghost shape and half an open mouth on the folded side of the paper. Carefully cut through all the layers, taking <u>out</u> the shaded areas shown. The arms and bottom part of the ghost should still be linked together when you open UP the paper chain.

Be careful with scissors and always cut away from your fingers.

Next, DRAW on the EYES when you open the chain. To make a longer chain, stick more ghosts together.

By changing the shape you cut out, you can make snowmen, Christmas trees and lots of different types of paper chains. ENJOY!

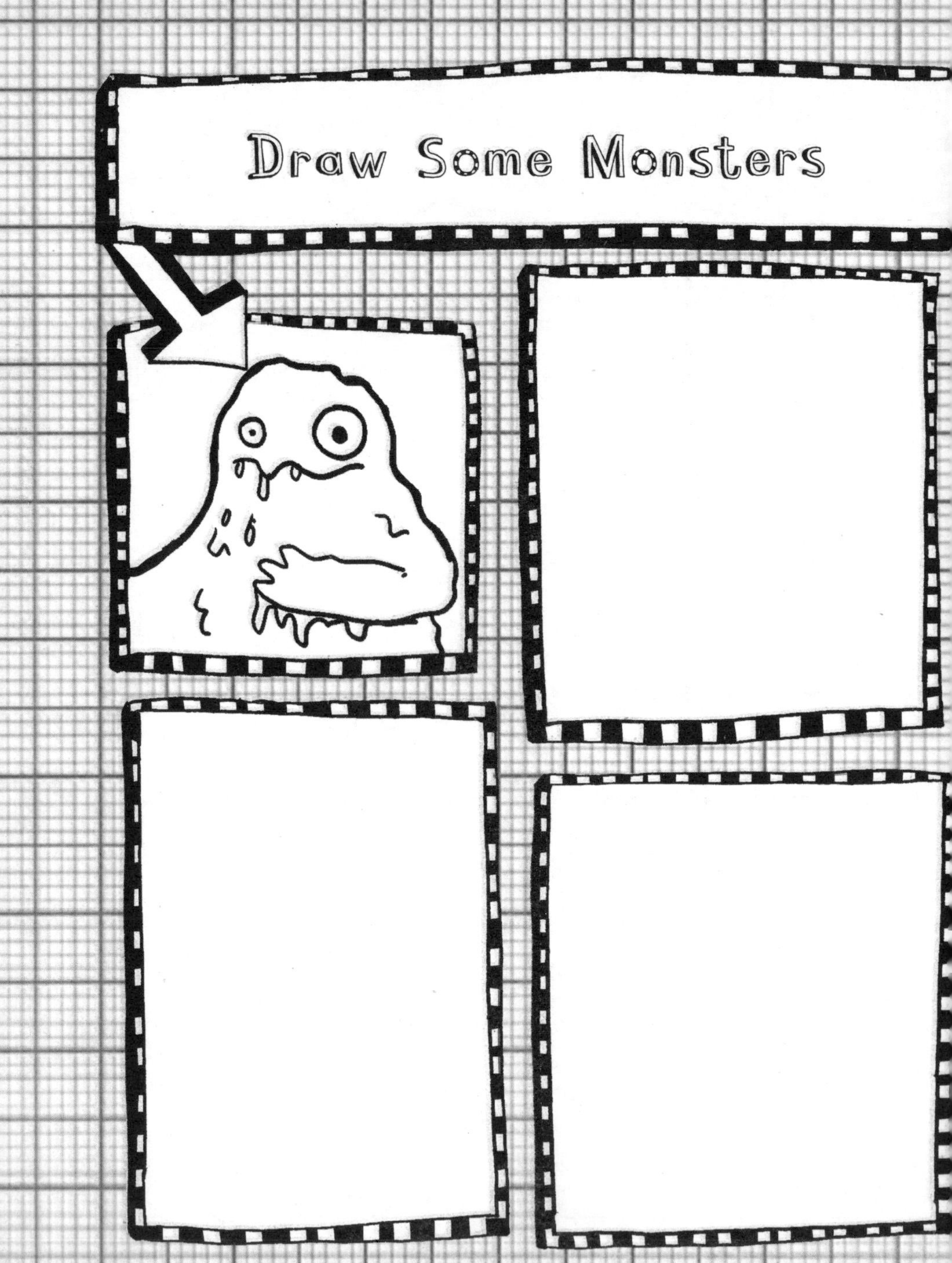
Draw Some Monsters

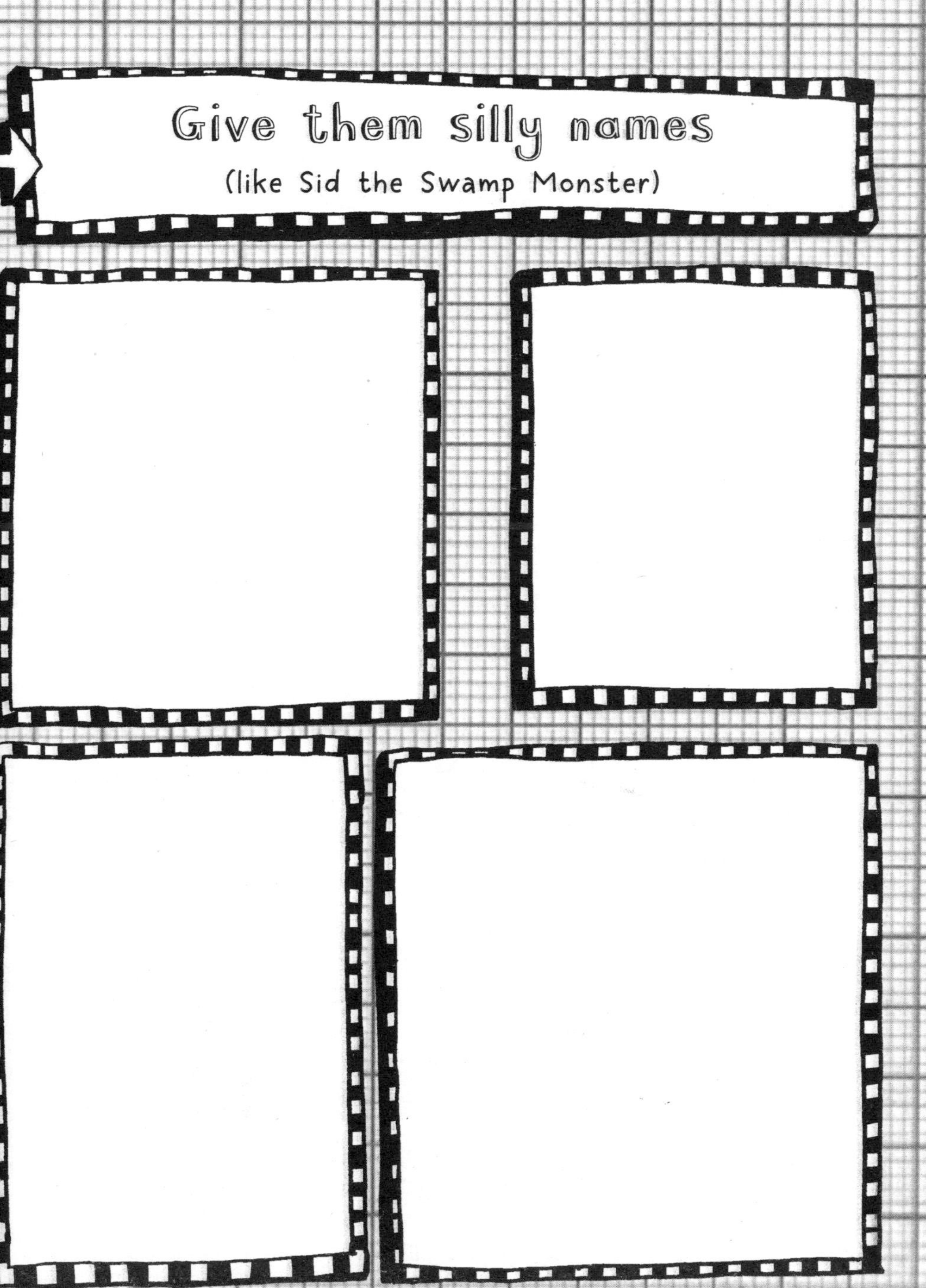
Give them silly names
(like Sid the Swamp Monster)

WRITE down FUNNY words that make you LAUGH.
Grumble wobble
VERY funny, Tom...
Silly sausage
TOM

Draw more LAUGHING faces.

# What ARE they SAYING?

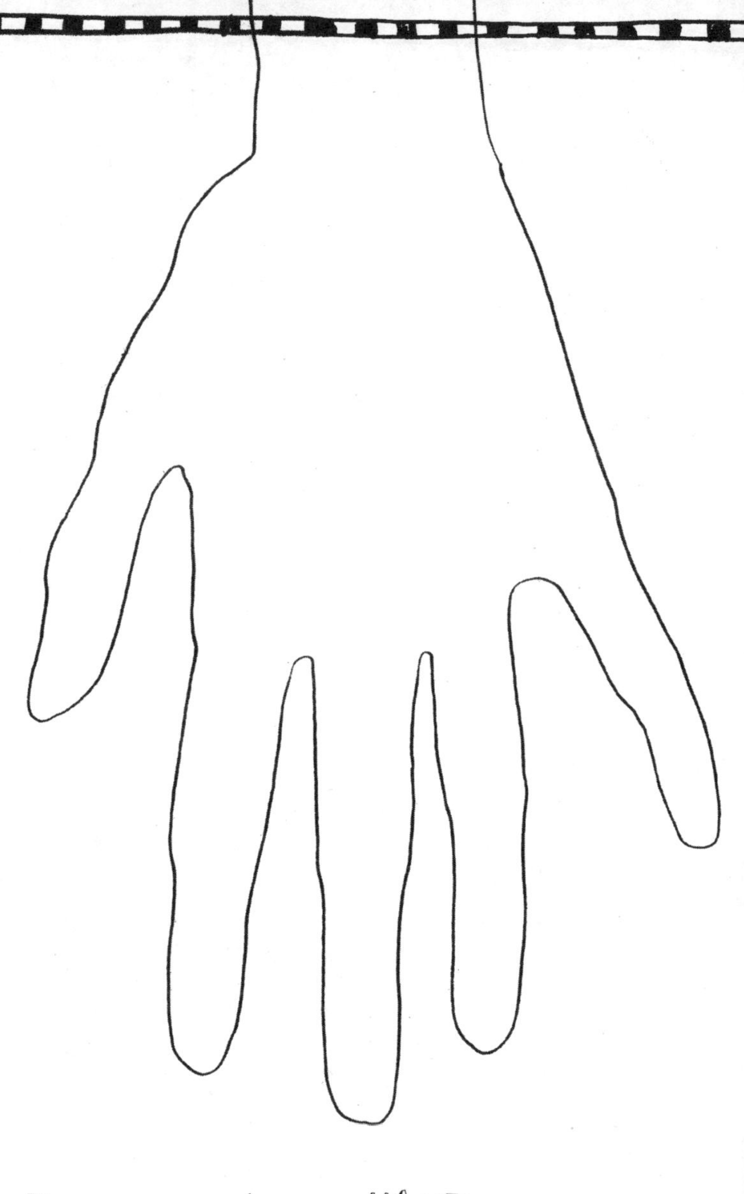

Draw around your HAND
and turn it into something ELSE.

Page to draw around your HAND

WRITE YOUR OWN POEM

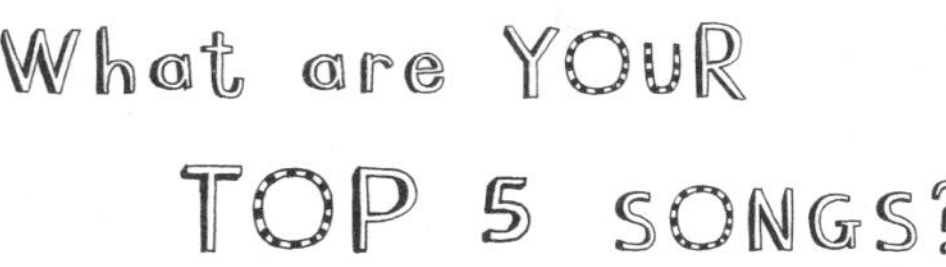


TOP
5

1

2

3

4

5

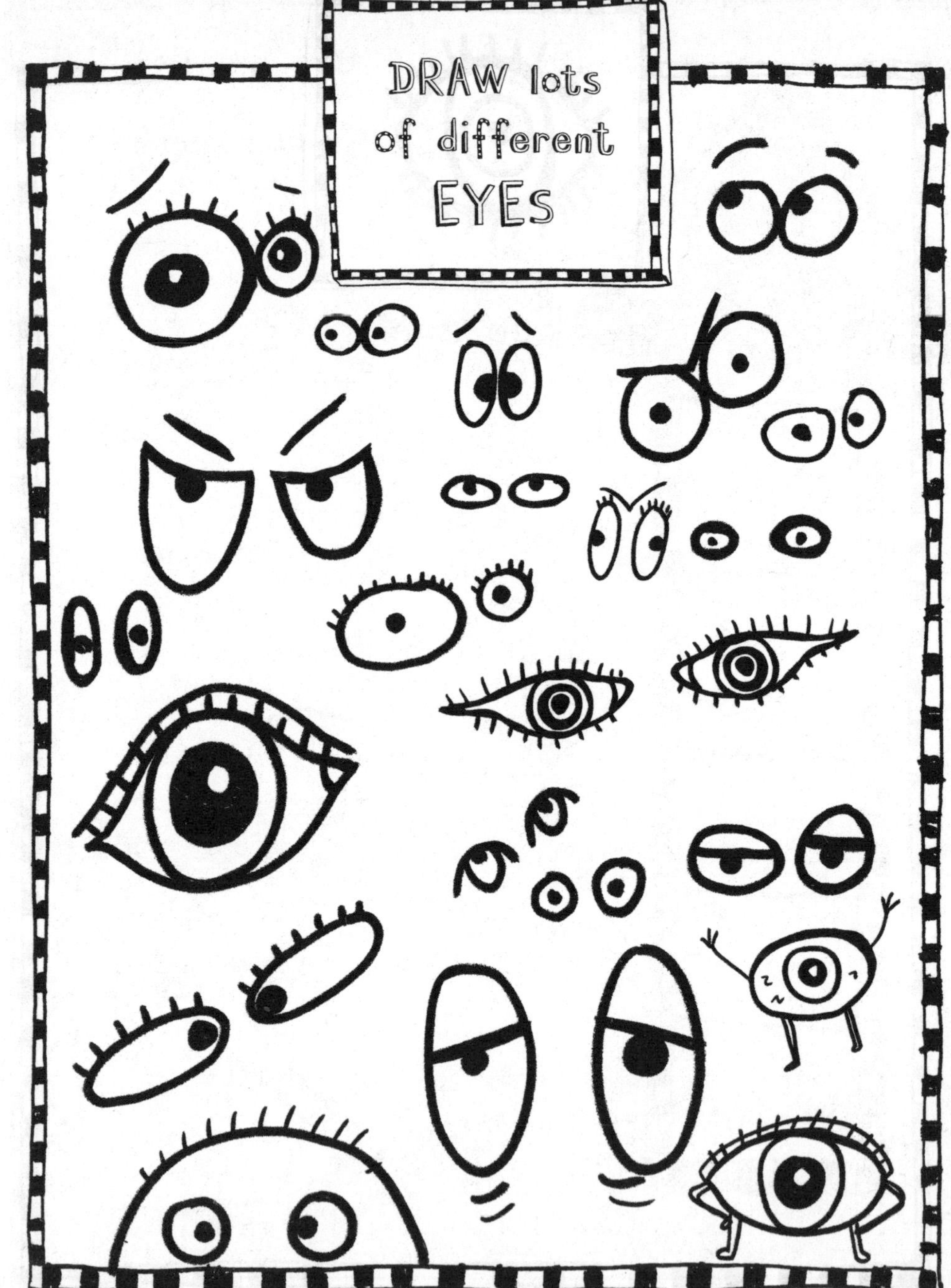
DRAW lots
of different
EYEs

Eye eye

Fill with colour

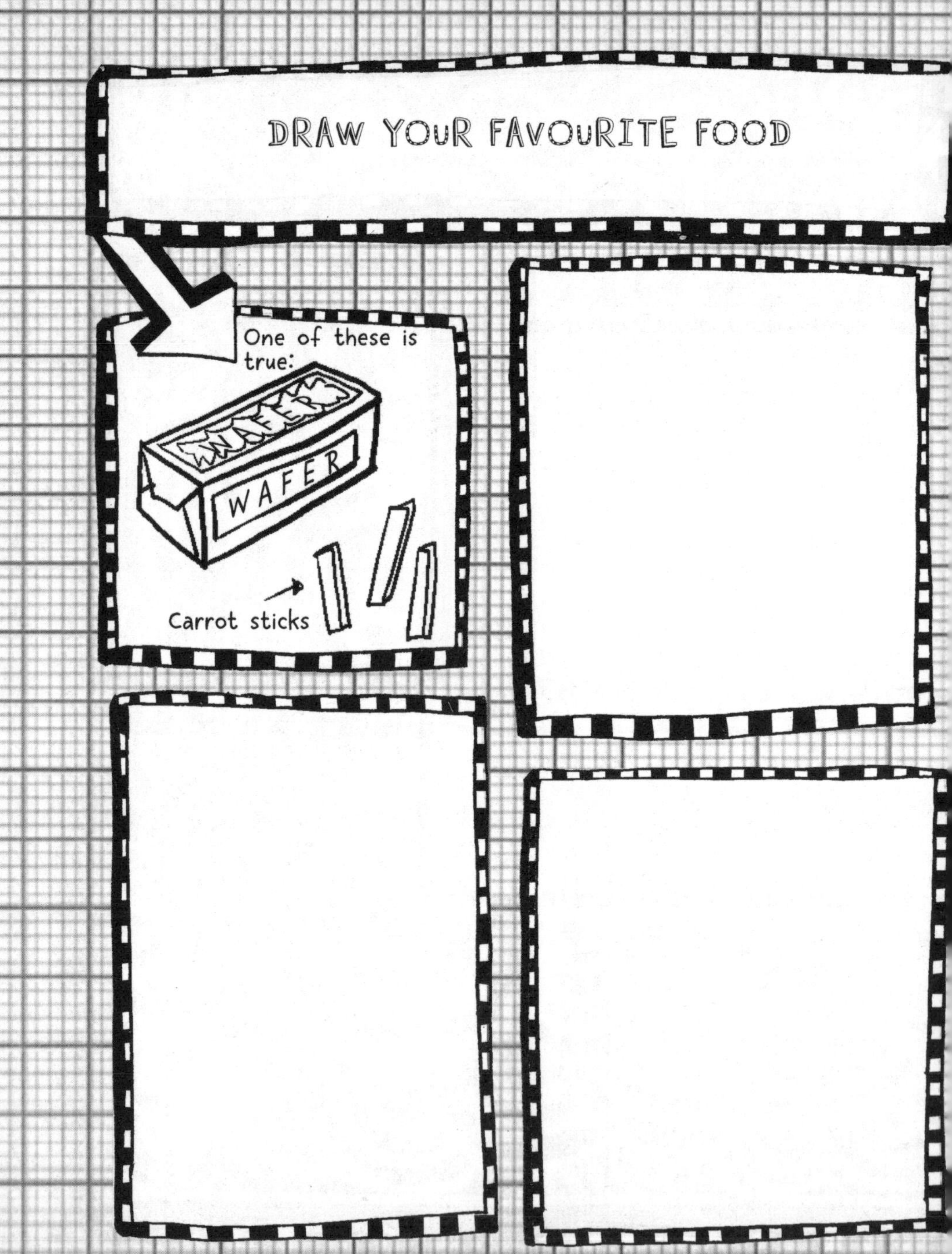
DRAW YOUR FAVOURITE FOOD
One of these is true:
WAFER
WAFER
WAFER
Carrot sticks

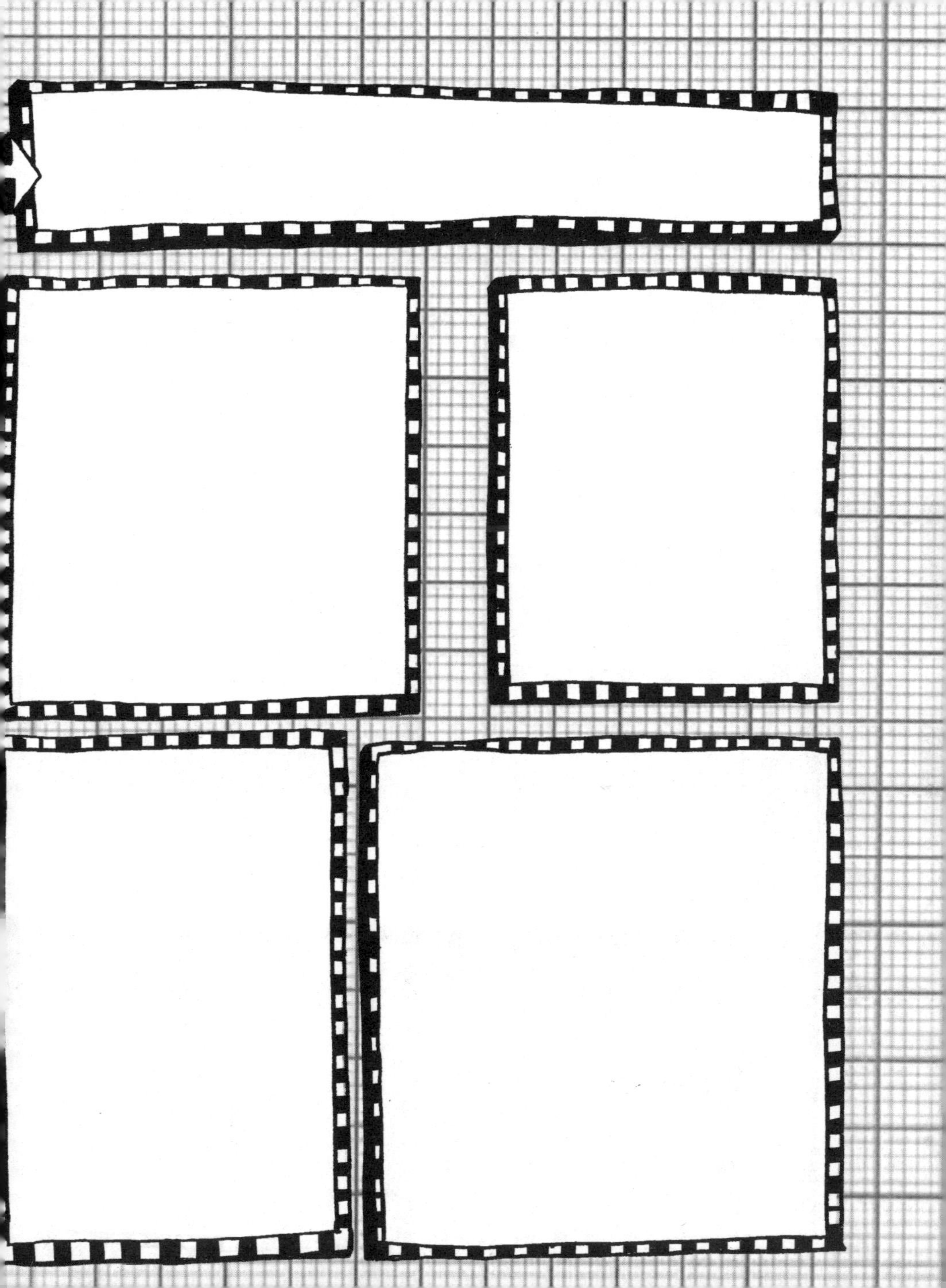

Write
A BIG
MESSAGE

# Scribble a Picture

Delia is surrounded by...

# What is Delia standing on?

STICK photos
of anything and
EVERYTHING
on these pages.
(Do write WHEN,
WHERE, WHO is
in the photo.
You WILL forget!)

What's that?

WINTER
Cold, Cheese and
DogZombies

Band practice today?
I'll bring SNACKS! Yes!
In the GARAGE
I still can't play - my hands won't move!
My keyboard has ICE! Oh no...
cold breath
cold bark
DOGZombies arrive.
Ready to practise? I have snacks.
PUFFS
It's so cold I can see my breath.
I can see my breath too!
Oh, yeah! Look!
Jumping!
OK.
WOOF!

rrr
It's freezing!
Brrrrrr
These gloves don't work...
My glasses are FROZEN!
My
eth are
attering.
Blocks of ICE
SNAP
Even my hair's cold!
We STILL need to practise, don't we?
le
o.
OK.
We should!
Practice makes perfect.
Derek! There's hot chocolate HERE!
Yes!
Band practice later?
Yes!
Sure.
Mmmm.
To be continued...

Band practice didn't exactly go to plan.

Who knew it would be THAT hard to play our instruments in the COLD "and with gloves on?"

Drinking hot chocolate to warm up has helped a LOT, but we still haven't done much practising. (None, to be exact.)

"After we've finished our hot chocolate shall we go back and have another go?" I suggest to Norman, Leroy and Derek.

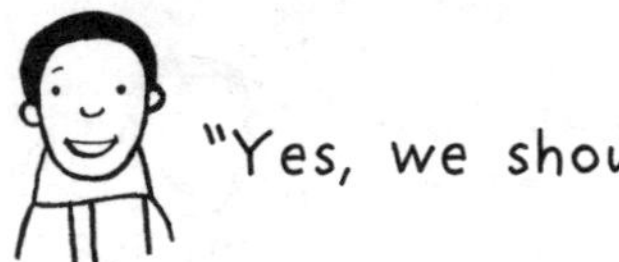

"Yes, we should," Leroy agrees.

"We need to write a new song as well," Derek reminds us.

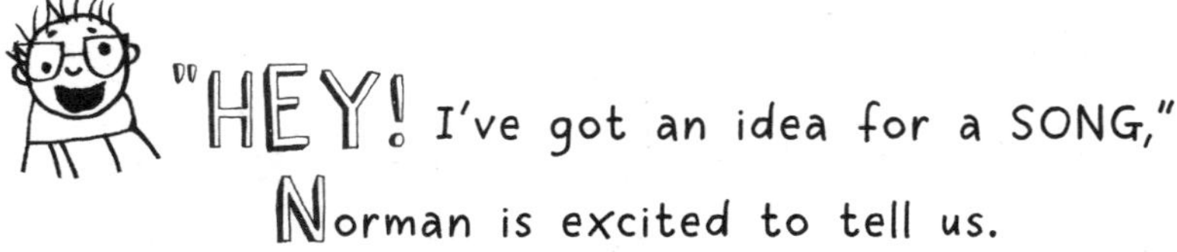

"HEY! I've got an idea for a SONG," Norman is excited to tell us.

"GREAT! What's it about?" I ask.

"CHEESE – and how much I like it," Norman says.

(This is not a surprise as Norman is always talking about cheese.)

"Shall I sing it for you?" he adds.

Me and Derek say no, but Leroy says, "LET'S hear it then."

Norman puts down his hot chocolate and stands in front of us and the TV. He's very STILL before he starts. And then...

Cheese! Cheese!
Cheese! Cheese!
Cheese for me!
Cheese for you!
I've got cheese,
Enough for two.
Guitar solo here
Cheese is TASTY!
Cheese is nice!
I like cheese as much as MICE!
Cheese! Cheese!
Say "Cheese Please..."

Norman's cheese song is unexpectedly catchy.

"What do you think?"

Norman wants to know.

"It's a cheese CLASSIC," I say.

"I don't even like cheese and I could sing this song," Leroy adds.

"I've got CHEESE stuck in my head. Yes please – to cheese," Derek tells Norman, who seems happy.

"Do mice really like cheese?" I ask.

"They do – and they like chocolate too," Norman tells me.

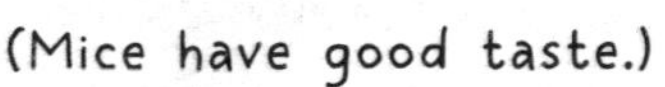

(Mice have good taste.)

Norman asks us a RANDOM question.

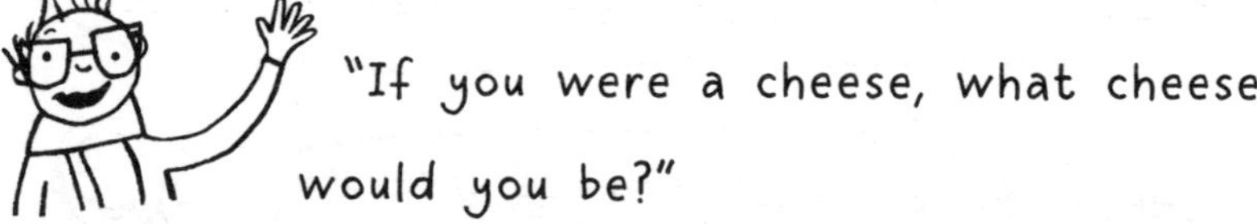

"If you were a cheese, what cheese would you be?"

(This gets us thinking.)

Eventually I say ... "A cheese triangle!"

Leroy doesn't like cheese so he says,

Cheese ... CAKE!

I'd be CHEDDAR – shall we go back to band practice?

Derek suggests before Norman starts going off on one.

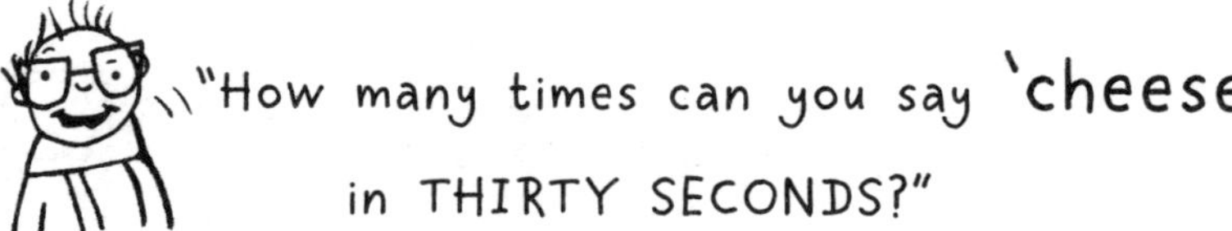

"How many times can you say 'cheese' in THIRTY SECONDS?"

We all take this as a CHALLENGE.

Derek has a stopwatch on his phone as we each have a go.

Cheese cheese CHEESE cheese cheese cheese
Cheese CHEESE CHEESE cheese cheese cheeeeee

CHEESE CHEESE cheese cheese cheeeeee
Cheese cheese cheese cheese

CHEESE CHEESE CHEESE CHEESE
Cheese cheese cheese cheese cheese cheeeeeese

Cheese cheese CHEESE cheese cheese cheese CHEESE
Cheese CHEESE CHEESE cheese cheese cheeeeee
Cheese cheese cheese cheese cheese

Norman is easily the winner, with Leroy a close second. This game takes a while and we should really get back to band practice.

"I've warmed up now," Leroy says.

"Let's go then," Derek agrees.

It's important for DOGZOMBIES to keep practising all our songs if we want to be the best band EVER...

But then...

Derek's dad calls out.

(There's always tomorrow.)

SPACE FOR YOUR OWN STORY

# DRAW PICTURES to GO with YOUR STORY

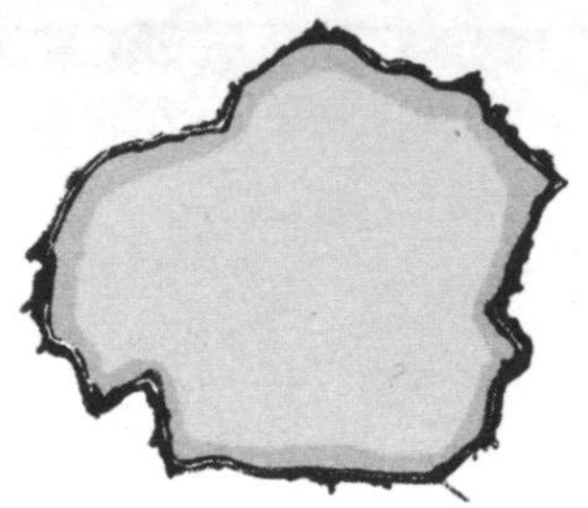

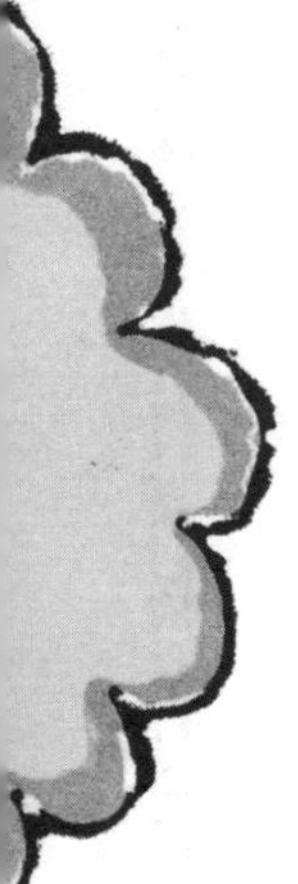

What has eaten
the page?

WHAT IS TOM THINKING ABOUT?
TOM

WHAT ARE YOU THINKING ABOUT?
me →
Date:

# FILL WITH (more) SNOW

# PUSH THOSE STRIPES

Press down using this end
Use the END of a thin paintbrush, or a blunt pencil to make marks on the paper. PRESS DOWN as HARD as you can. Then with the SIDE of a dark pencil, colour over the top of the marks.
They should stay white – like this --->
The deeper you make the marks in the paper, the more they'll stand out.
Now use the BLANK page to EXPERIMENT!
Use the SIDE of a dark pencil.

# Rooster needs a SNACK

(or two, or three).

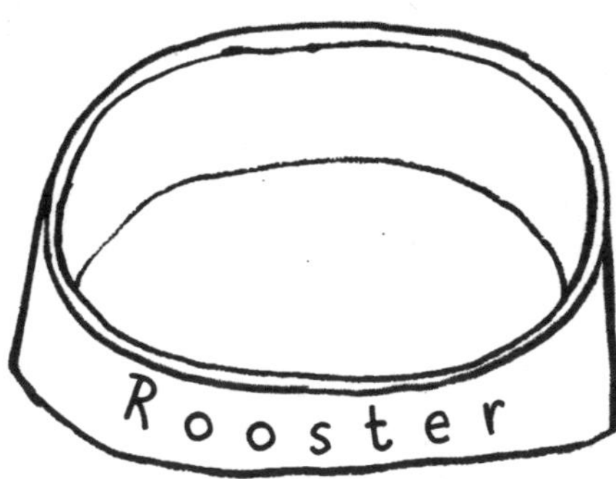

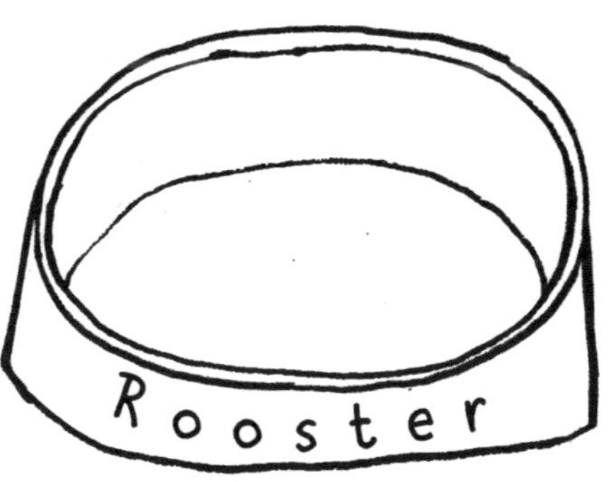
Rooster

FREE

STYLE

# TURN THESE NUMBERS INTO MONSTERS

1

2

3

4

5

I am
not a
number

# HATS PLEASE

MAKE a CARD
Fold an A4 piece of thin card in half.
Sketch out your design.
HAPPY BIRTHDAY
You can use some of the doodles on the opposite page to copy on to your card OR make up your own design for a birthday, thank you, or even a Christmas card.

Happy Birthday

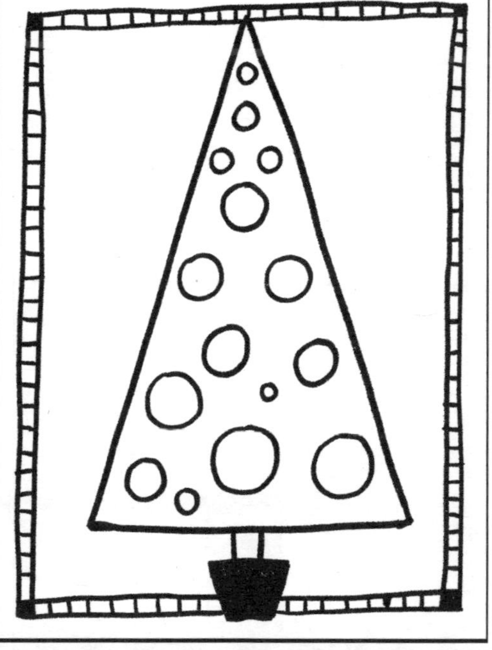

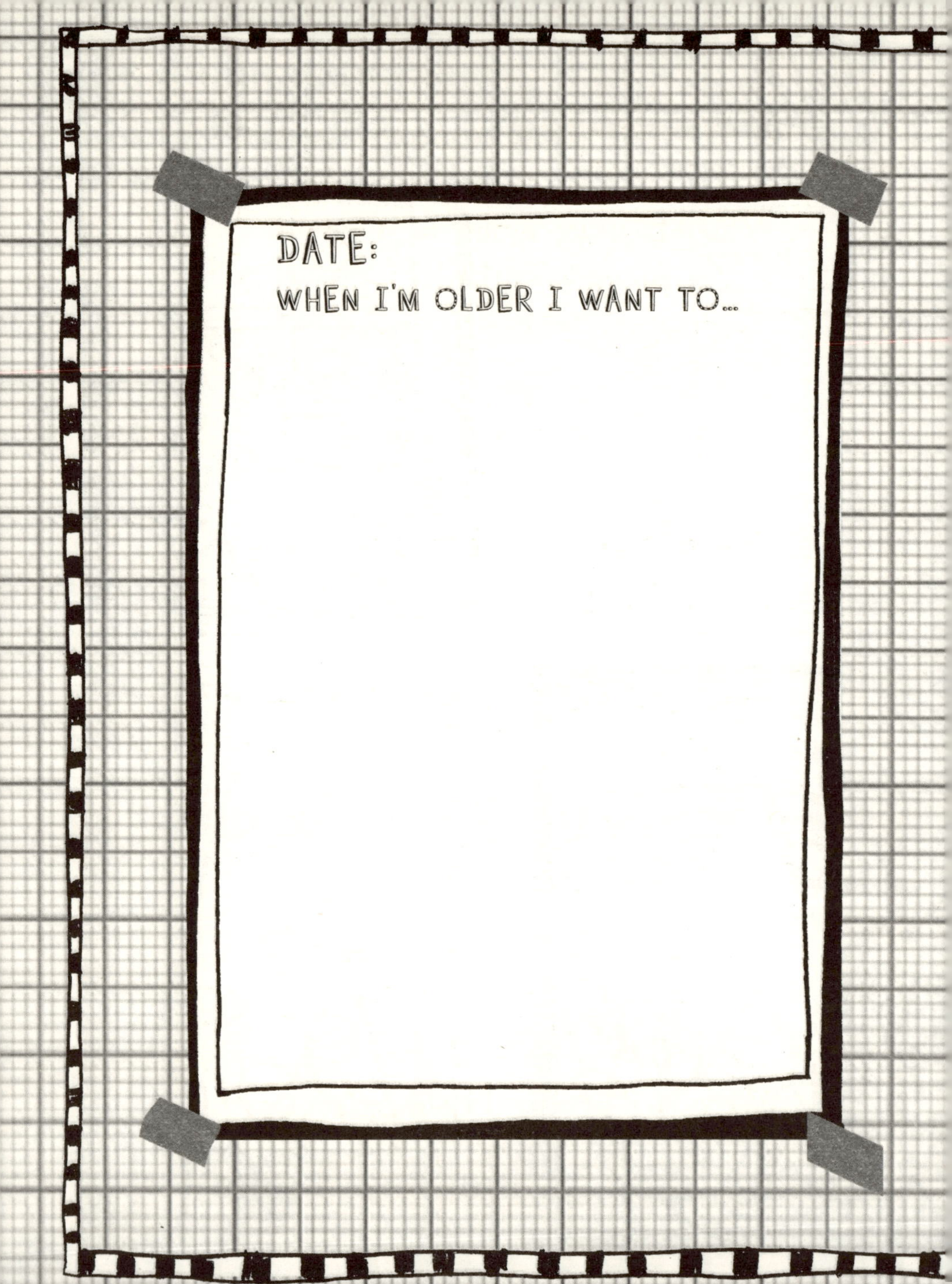
DATE:
WHEN I'M OLDER I WANT TO...

hello
WRITE your name in a very fancy way HERE:
Fancy pen
Amy Porter

Draw a very funny MUG.

Draw a not-so-funny MUG.

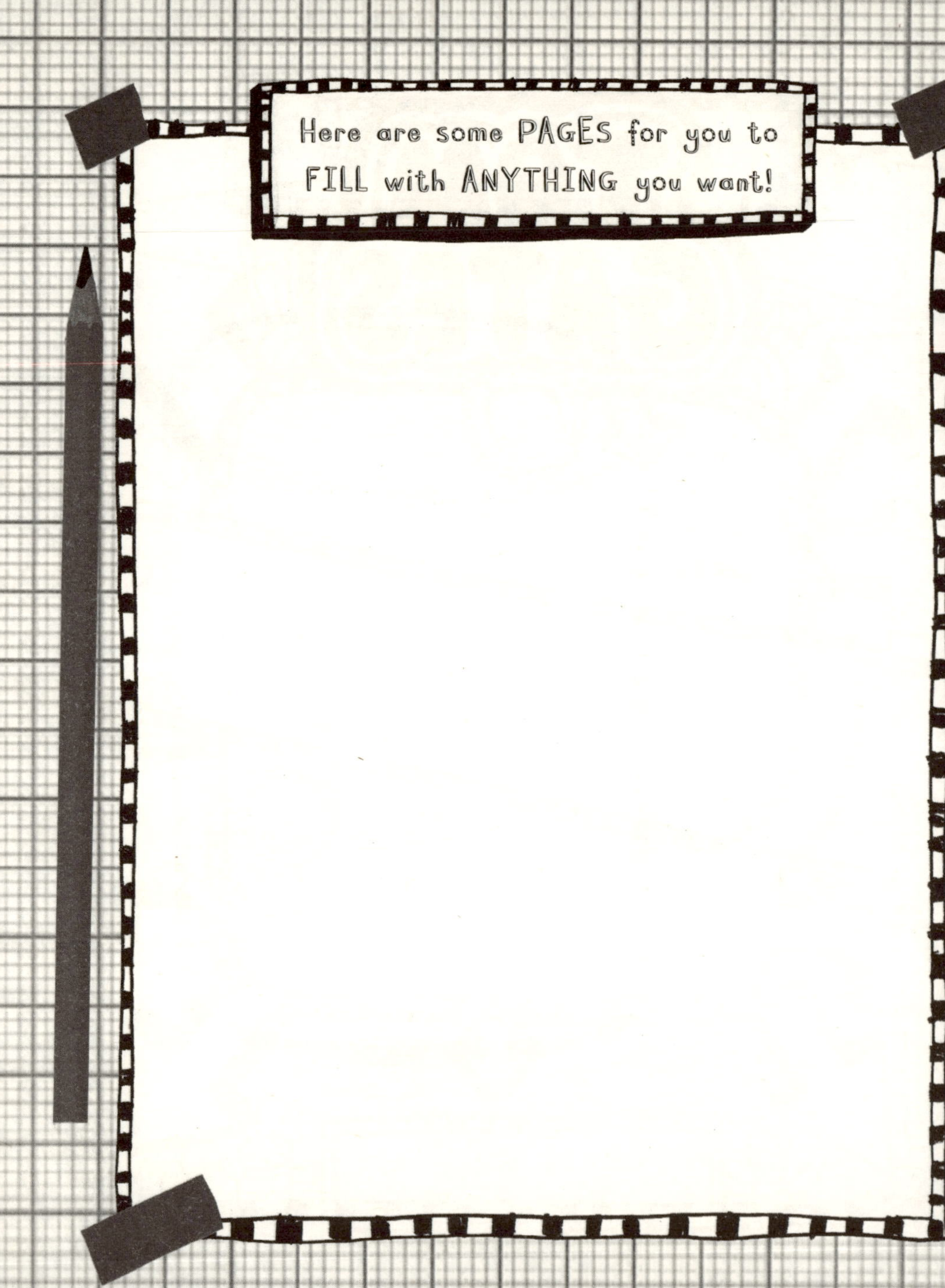
Here are some PAGES for you to
FILL with ANYTHING you want!

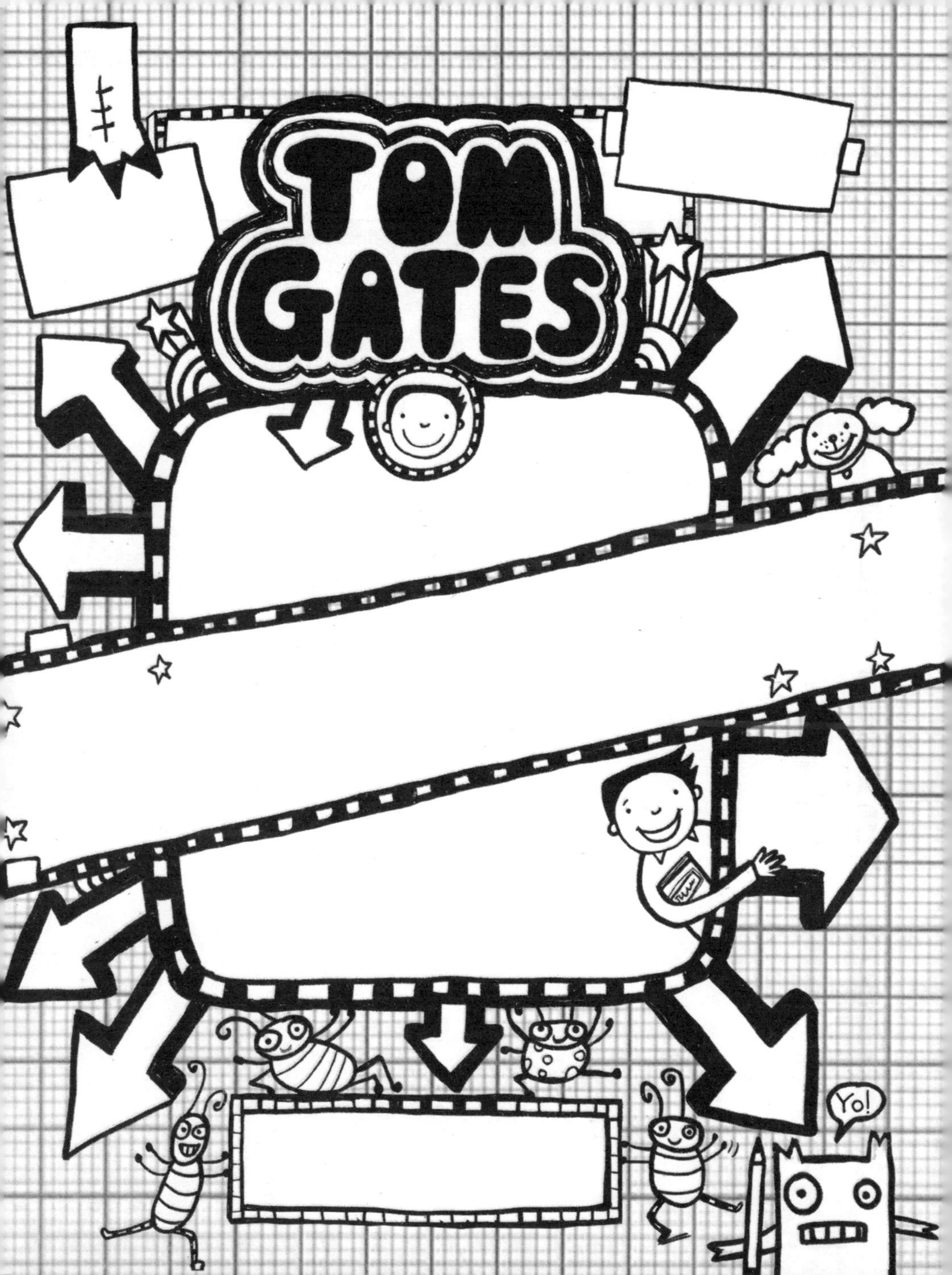

TOM GATES
Yo!

HERE'S where the FOUR-LEAF CLOVERS ARE!

There are actually 12 four-leaf clovers!

I FOUND ALL 7 of them!

LOOK! Here's the whole
Tom Gates collection.
How many have you read?
TOM GATES
The BRILLIANT WORLd OF TOM GATES
BY LIZ PICHON
TOM GATES
EXcellent ExCUSES
(and other good stuff)
BY LIZ PICHON
TOM GATES
Everything's AMAZING
(sort of)
BY LIZ PICHON
TOM GATES
GENIUS IDEAS
(mostly)
BY LIZ PICHON
TOM GATES
Absolutely FANTASTIC
(at SOME things)
BY LIZ PICHON
TOM GATES
EXTRA SPECIAL TREATS
(not)
BY LIZ PICHON
TOM GATES
A tiny Bit LUCKY
BY LIZ PICHON
TOM GATES
YES! NO. (Maybe...)
BY LIZ PICHON
TOM GATES
TOP of the CLASS
BY LIZ PICHON
TOM GATES
SUPER GOOD SKILLS
(almost)
BY LIZ PICHON
TOM GATES
DOG ZOMBIES RULE
(for now)
BY LIZ PICHON

www.thebrilliantworldoftomgates.com

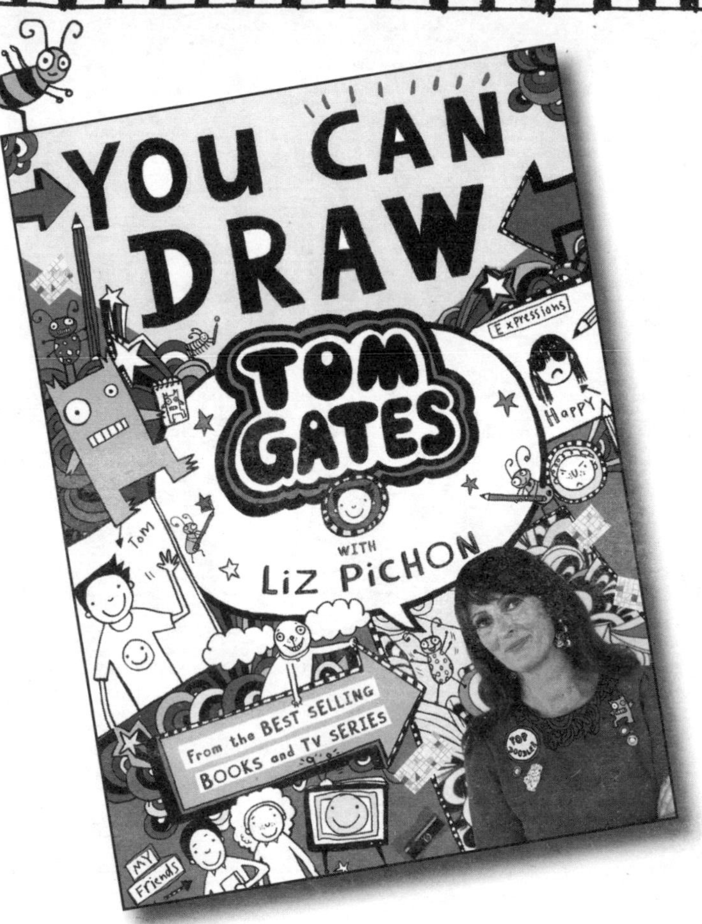


Learn to draw step-by-step people, places and objects from Tom's world.

The must-have art activity book for fans of Tom Gates.

With SONGS from the award-winning TV SHOW!

THE TOM GATES MUSIC BOOK

LEARN to strum and drum

FOR Guitar Ukulele Drums Vocals Piano Recorder

PLAY it!

PRACTISE with the TOM GATES music APP.

DOGZOMBIES

DUDE3

INSIDE: ALL the songs

Songs from the books by LIZ PICHON

From DOGZOMBIES to DUDE3, music is a HUGE part of the Tom Gates world. Learn how to play all your favourite songs from the series with REAL notation for:

- Guitar
- Piano
- Ukulele
- Recorder

And with notation for drums and tips and tricks for vocals!

Read all the Tom Gates books?
Well, now you can read ***SHOE WARS***,
a standalone adventure story.

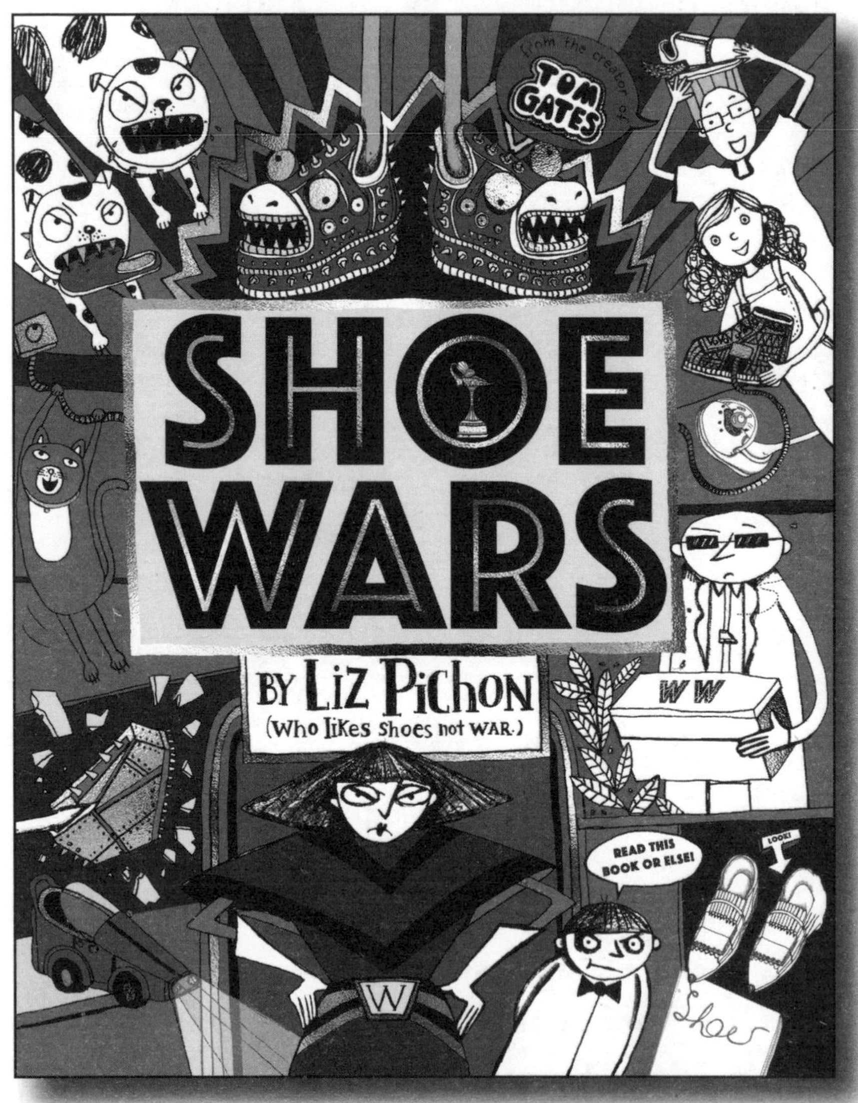

*A Sunday Times* Children's Book of the Year pick.

"Bursting with imagination and fabulous gadgets, ***Shoe Wars*** is full of Pichon's characteristic warmth, humour and quirky illustrations"
*The Bookseller*

"A tale oozing creativity and packed with pen and ink illustrations, exciting and expressive typography and visual jokes" *BookTrust*

Welcome to Shoe Town – and meet Ruby and Bear Foot. They are running out of time to rescue their inventor dad from his hideous boss, Wendy Wedge. She'll do ANYTHING to win the glitzy Golden Shoe Award and knows that entering flying shoes is her hot ticket to the trophy. Flying shoes that Ruby and Bear just happen to be hiding...

Liz Pichon is one of the UK's best-loved and bestselling creators of children's books.

Her TOM GATES series has been translated into 45 languages, sold millions of copies worldwide, and has won the Roald Dahl Funny Prize, the Blue Peter Book Award for Best Story and the younger fiction category of the Waterstones Children's Book Prize.

In the eleven years since THE BRILLIANT WORLD OF TOM GATES first published, the books have inspired the nation's children to get creative, whether that's through reading, drawing, doodling, writing, making music or performing.

"I wanted to FILL the books with ALL the things I loved doing when I was a kid. It's just the best feeling ever to know children are enjoying reading the books, because I love making them. So thank you so much for choosing Tom Gates and keep reading and doodling!"

Visit Liz at www.lizpichon.com

(School photo of Liz being gr